Human Rights Rhetoric

Rhetoric scholars have articulated diverse approaches to both civil and human rights as political, ethical, and academic discourses. *Human Rights Rhetoric: Traditions of Testifying and Witnessing* initiates important interdisciplinary conversations within human rights rhetoric concerning the construction of rights knowledge, the role of advocacy, and politics of representations during acts of witnessing. Developing a conceptual framework for rhetorical inquiry into rights discourse, the collection of essays by established scholars demonstrates a range of approaches and subject matter. From textual analysis of AIDS politics and activism to theoretical discussions of the nature of rights rhetoric and confession, the book challenges many current assumptions about rights history and practices and still provides an introduction to the recent themes for classroom use. To encourage critical reflection on the assumptions, contentions, and implications of political representations and human rights, the editors have concluded the collection with a series of suggestive visual works without comment to prompt viewers' own engagement with them.

This book was originally published as a special issue of *Rhetoric Society Quarterly.*

Arabella Lyon has published recent essays on comparative rhetoric, human rights, and Chinese communication in *Philosophy and Rhetoric*, *College English*, *Composition and Communication*, and *Ancient Non-Greek Rhetorics.* Her book *Intentions: Negotiated, Contested, and Ignored* won the Ross Winterowd Award for the Outstanding Book in Rhetoric and Composition. Currently she is completing a manuscript entitled 'Deliberative Acts: Democracy, Rhetoric, and Rights'.

Lester C. Olson's books include *Emblems of American Community in the Revolutionary Era* (1991), *Benjamin Franklin's Vision of American Community* (2004), and, with co-editors Cara A. Finnegan and Diane S. Hope, *Visual Rhetoric* (2007). His essays concerning Audre Lorde's advocacy appear in the *Quarterly Journal of Speech*, *Philosophy & Rhetoric*, *American Voices*, *Queering Public Address*, and *The Responsibilities of Rhetoric*.

Human Rights Rhetoric
Traditions of Testifying and Witnessing

Edited by
Arabella Lyon & Lester C. Olson

Routledge
Taylor & Francis Group
LONDON AND NEW YORK

RHETORIC SOCIETY QUARTERLY

First published 2012
by Routledge
2 Park Square, Milton Park, Abingdon, Oxon, OX14 4RN

Simultaneously published in the USA and Canada
by Routledge
711 Third Avenue, New York, NY 10017

Routledge is an imprint of the Taylor & Francis Group, an informa business

This book is a reproduction of *Rhetoric Society Quarterly*, vol. 41, issue 3. The Publisher requests to those authors who may be citing this book to state, also, the bibliographical details of the special issue on which the book was based.

British Library Cataloguing in Publication Data
A catalogue record for this book is available from the British Library

ISBN13: 978-0-415-50838-4 (h/b)

Typeset in New Times Roman
by Taylor & Francis Books

Publisher's Note
The publisher would like to make readers aware that the chapters in this book may be referred to as articles as they are identical to the articles published in the special issue. The publisher accepts responsibility for any inconsistencies that may have arisen in the course of preparing this volume for print.

Contents

Human Rights Rhetoric: Traditions of Testifying and Witnessing

Arabella Lyon & Lester C. Olson[1]

Rhetoric scholars have developed approaches to both civil and human rights as political, ethical, and academic discourses. Such approaches include examining the development and reproduction of hierarchies, the politics of representation, and the relationships among symbols, audiences consisting of disparate communities, rights, and rights events. After an overview of rhetorical contributions, as well as risks and limitations of a rhetoric approach to human rights, this introduction turns to the focus of the special issue: testifying and witnessing as a way to scrutinize the roles of bystanders to rights atrocities and the responses of listeners who may be rights committed or not.

Human rights, exemplified by the Universal Declaration of Human Rights (1948), have become a key term in international politics and rhetoric after the Cold War. Consequently, "human rights" and "civil rights" have been declared, recognized, re-affirmed, assaulted, and actively undermined around the globe. As Michael Ignatieff asserts, "human rights has become the dominant moral vocabulary in foreign affairs" (29). Human rights discourse, moreover, has become a dominant academic vocabulary. Search the keyword "human rights" in a research university library, and over nine thousand books come up, the vast majority published since 2000. The ramifications of human rights discourse encompass such abiding subjects and intense controversies as civil rights, positive and negative rights, declarations of universal and cultural or local rights, public advocacy from nongovernmental organizations (NGOs), independent documentaries and grassroots

[1]The co-editors have contributed equally to this special issue.

uprisings, statements concerning the appropriate use of legal force and representation, as well as the diplomatic milestones articulated in formal covenants or treaties and dramatic media spectacles portraying engagements by international bodies.

Even so, the meaning of "human rights" and "civil rights" has been the subject of public controversies and, in fact, varies across cultures. Public controversies have centered on such basic, open-ended questions as: What are human rights? What principles and reciprocal commitments, if any, should communities around the globe be obligated to recognize as fundamental human rights? From what spiritual, ethical, and/or political sources have communities derived diverse conceptions of human rights? Are certain human rights so fundamental as to be "universal," as the United Nations proclaimed in 1948? Does this ostensibly "universal" character of human rights mean that certain human rights principles can never be compromised and, if so, how have communities dealt constructively with collisions among conflicting human rights? (e.g., contrast Eleanor Roosevelt's and Elizabeth Kiss's speeches concerning compromise.) Basic questions such as these suggest that, as a discipline, rhetoric could contribute to ongoing conversations, arguments, and debates about the ramifications of human rights representation for public life.

Within disciplinary rhetoric, human rights theory and criticism have developed sufficiently for disciplinary conversations. In fact, rhetoric is uniquely positioned to offer particular insights into the language of human rights declarations, covenants, and the symbolic action of human rights claims, laws, norms, aspirations, and deliberations. Among the more robust areas which interest rhetoricians are the genres of human rights discourse, particularly narrative types, as well as the politics of representation within written and visual texts. Although the nature of representation is not so easily separated from the formal issues of genre, an emphasis on the political context makes studies of representation particularly pertinent. In addition to concerns with how rights are represented, traditions of rhetoric offer a way into discussing reception. How do audiences identify with rights and individuals whose rights have been violated? How might a particular audience be moved to action? Rhetoric and communication's traditional concern with contingency and truth also enables rhetoric scholars to offer unique and significant insights into human rights debates. For instance, given the legal, juridical, and political nature of human rights debates, inquiries on the nature of truth and the importance of contingencies—that is, questions of "what really happened"—are familiar to rhetoric and communication scholars.

This brief introduction explores what might be considered a rhetorical approach to human rights in that it articulates a rationale for examining how rights are represented in language and symbolism, how advocates construct particular responses in contingent situations, and how public debates influence communities, interpretations of rights, and rights enforcement (for alternatives, e.g., see Cmiel, Hope). Then, it turns to the specific focus of this special issue on witnessing and testifying to examine one focal point for such an approach to human rights. In providing a collection of original essays by accomplished rhetoric scholars from a variety of backgrounds, the special issue will promote and strengthen ongoing conversations concerning communication and human rights. Each essay will address witnessing and testimony as an aspect of human rights rhetoric in the United States and international settings. To encourage critical reflection on the assumptions, contentions, and implications of political representations and human rights, we have added a series of visual works at the conclusion without comment to prompt viewers' own engagement with them. These images are not meant to be exhaustive, simply suggestive.

In general, a rhetorical approach to human rights considers the human rights implications of language and symbolism by examining the hierarchical significance of words, definitions, re-definitions, symbols designating social groupings, myths, rituals, symbolic images, and the like. In other words, a rhetorical approach to human rights documents, debates, and artifacts scrutinizes symbolic actions constructing identifications and divisions among individuals and social groups (Burke *A Rhetoric* esp. xiii–xiv, 19–29), and it examines the development and reproduction of hierarchies—political power, economic resources, social privilege (Bourdieu). Rhetorical inquiry into human rights discourses examines the politics of representation in establishing, maintaining, and transforming hierarchies in social, political, legal, and economic forums. Concerned with how language is adapted to circumstance, rhetorical inquiry examines how audiences identify with both rights themselves and the individuals or communities whose rights have been violated. Most significantly, rhetorical analyses of human rights attend to rhetorical processes, forms, and concepts in representing or portraying human rights concerns—exemplified by double-binds, performatives, enactment, narrative and myth, rhetorical appeals such as character (ethos), emotions (pathos) and reasoning (logos), argument, expert and lay testimony, as well as the nature of embodiment and otherness.

The attention to double binds accompanies even so basic a rhetorical focus as the scrutiny of language itself (Jamieson), as in Adrienne Rich's insight, "This is the oppressor's language, but I need it to speak to you" (364). Rich joins other twentieth-century activist-scholars, such as Daly, Davis, and Dworkin, in underscoring how the very means of communication can work against advocates' endeavors to actualize social justice. Rich and other likeminded activist-scholars' observation during the 1970s has become a topoi in contemporary rights criticism (e.g., Doxtader, Gilmore, Hasian, *Rhetorical Vectors*, Hasian, *In the Name*, Hesford and Kozol, Schaeffer and Smith). In addition, her observation underscores certain challenges in using language and symbols to transform cultures in life-enhancing ways, including witnessing and testifying, because the systems of representation reflect the histories of domination and power within them. Human rights can be declared, advocated, and debated only through symbolic representations, however much these vary among cultures. Thus, Rich's concern about the inheritance of oppressive language informs even milestones in the history of human rights (e.g., provisions in the Magna Charta concerning the use of testimony by a woman or, in UN's Universal Declaration, language that by today's standards is sexist in the usage of the generic "he").

Declarations of rights, such as the UN's Universal Declaration, tend to affirm in public life the aspirations, ideals, or standards that members of communities expect reciprocally of themselves and each other. At times these guidelines are translated, however fallibly, into national and international laws, whose enforcement depends on political will and commitments of material resources (Whalen). Viewed narrowly as legal obligations or frameworks, human rights discourses, at times, are viewed skeptically as tools by which elites manage or control otherwise already disenfranchised or marginalized, ostensibly "autonomous" individuals and other communities—oftentimes behind a persona or mask of beneficence. However, at the same time, broad-based, grassroots organizers, advocates, and educators from within disenfranchised communities, at times, find human rights vocabularies to be powerful resources for revealing hypocrisy, making radical claims on elites for recognition, inclusion, and justice within communities, and affirming their stature as fully human within dehumanizing and oppressive cultures.

The risks and limits of a rhetorical approach to human rights fall into three broad categories: (1) a limited perspective on language and symbolism rather than their entwined relationship to material and historical conditions that clearly extend beyond such representations; (2) a concealment of relationships of power, privilege, and resourcefulness within considerations of idealism; and (3) a delusion of ethical work in simply pursuing certain academic interests and labor. First, a focus on the representations and "human" in general combine to risk obscuring the effect of differential treatment, bodily experiences, and histories of diverse groups through such social mechanisms as legislation, religious codes, and legal decisions, as well as bodily performances and social habits (e.g., the institution of slavery in the United States had different symbolic, bodily, and material ramifications for white and black people, while marriage laws have differing ramifications for the sexes as well as gay and lesbian people). By focusing on legislation, judicial codes and legal decisions, as well as bodily performances and symbolic artifacts, rhetoric may fail to acknowledge the corporeal body and the rights to material conditions for human survival. In other words, consequential sociological, psychological, legal, and medical dimensions of human-rights struggles ought not to be reduced to representations or rhetoric.

Still further risks and limitations attend the study of ethics and idealism in society. Rhetoric scholars might recall that for Nietzsche and other intellectuals a preoccupation with ethics has sometimes been considered a form of delusion covering terms for relations of power (e.g., Alcoff, Ballengee, Hesford and Kozol, Kennedy, Merry, Stiehm). And yet, evoking familiar human-rights standards has mobilized extraordinary power and resources in ways that warrant skepticism about simplistic alternatives between the ideal and ethical on the one hand or the practical matters of power and resources on the other.

Finally, certain forms of academic labor can actually deflect people's attention from human rights. And yet, other varieties of academic work have circumscribed value in that they raise awareness of human rights concerns, provide intellectual equipment for engaging them, and have the potential for scholars as public intellectuals to contribute to the broader community's concerns with social justice. In short, the qualities of academic labor vary widely in their implications for human rights both within and beyond national boundaries.

Rhetoric scholars are well positioned to learn from and contribute to ongoing human rights controversies, responding to questions such as: What is an ethical approach to representing and responding to rights violations? How might advocates, communities, and nations best use language and communication technologies to intervene when dealing with human rights atrocities? Indeed, whether and how to intervene can be a dilemma to people who wish to present themselves or their community as advocates or protectors of "human rights." Although the United States has often portrayed itself as the "protector" of human rights around the world, in recent years the United States has been condemned internationally for alleged human-rights violations, ranging from torture and sexual abuse to illegal wiretapping and invasions of privacy, all in the name of human security—a fundamental human right declared by the UN.

Yet, non-intervention can be profoundly problematic in certain other cases, too. Elie Wiesel poignantly reminds us in his public lecture, "The Perils of Indifference," that the silence and inaction of bystanders can be crucial factors in making human rights violations possible, such as those of the Holocaust. And yet, how bystanders do intervene, if at all, can introduce some complicated concerns about the "protector's" motivations, as Judith Hicks Stiehm has argued was the case in imagery portraying the "rape" of Kuwait. The promise and pitfalls attending the roles of those who witness and testify are complex and, at times, can be hazardous for already harmed individuals and communities, a factor which rhetoricians are well prepared to critique with attention to motives, since "protection" can be a euphemism for taking control, while "support," in contrast, can meaningfully enhance the agency of affected populations (e.g., see Alcoff, 24–27, on factors to consider when speaking for others).

This special issue concentrates primarily on witnessing and testifying as one way to scrutinize the problematic role of bystanders to human rights atrocities. Despite the pitfalls of reproducing oppression by employing inherited representations, both language and symbolism are a necessary means for asserting and advancing specific rights. For the purposes of the introduction, we use "witness" and "testify" interchangeably. Dictionary definitions do not vary significantly; both are defined as "bearing witness." In the extended definitions of their verb forms in the *Oxford English Dictionary*, "witness" connotes more of a physical experience of formally signing, swearing, seeing, and auditing. Though we are not making a significant distinction, others have. Rosetta E. Ross, in her discussion of black religious women's activism, defines testifying as speaking about God's work and witnessing as the following behavioral response to God's presence (223). In *Witnessing Slavery: The Development of Ante-bellum Slave Narratives*, Francis Smith Foster considers witnessing particularly, conceiving witnessing as less concerned with mimesis and historical accuracy and more engaged in "the power to reveal, to transform, and to transcend" (xx). Both theorists are concerned with the transcendence of a spoken and lived reality, the creation of a counter-discourse, and the creation of a different world, a common concern of witnesses.

In a 2010 NPR interview, Charles Bowden, author of *Murder City: Ciudad Juarez and the Global Economy's New Killing Fields*, is asked why he returns to Juarez: "What is the allure of the story, there, for you?" His reply reveals his commitment to a different world and many other tensions in witnessing:

> I don't really know allures. What I think is there have to be witnesses. What I think is a record has to be made. So, frankly, I don't want to cover this. I'd much rather go smell the coffee somewhere or go catch a trout. But I want—I think, I mean, 5000 people have been butchered in this city in three years. Somebody has to write this down. Somewhere there has to be a record.

His response reveals a relationship between the event itself and the witnessing of the event. If the event is terrible, the witness may not be part of the terror but may still feel compelled as an audience to respond and record the event. Witnessing is a decisive response to the question of trees falling in the forest. Someone has to hear, see, smell, touch, or even taste for the event to happen, at least for it to happen politically and rhetorically. The record must be made as a first step toward a political response, and yet there is anxiety about the influence and agency inherent in writing down the butchery. For witnessing and testifying to be a speech act, an act constituting a change by its utterance, the act must be received by a community of action (Austin 1–11; Bourdieu, 107–116); just as the "I do" at a wedding depends on the recognition of a community, just as the verdict of a jury depends on a judge's act, Bowden's record depends on a rights-committed audience who is willing to act through public rhetoric and commitment of resources.

Although there is an assumption that witnessing and testifying provide necessary information about human rights violations and that information will create advocates, public deliberations, even anger and outrage, these assumptions often are disproved by a lack of political engagement or consequences. Documentation, "somewhere," is important, but what is done with the documentation, the testifying during an NPR breakfast, is unclear. Even if a public is made aware of the violence, in what ways will bystanders respond? Will altruism characterize the bystanders' response, or indifference, complicity, and appropriation (McPhail "Complicity,"

McPhail "Politics," Matthison et al., Alcoff, Scott, Spelman, Mutua, Brown, Crenshaw)? What are the rhetorical effects of particular acts of witnessing and testifying? How does the effective witness induce cooperation, persuasion, and identification?

The speaking of violations occurs in multiple sites: aesthetic, political, legislative, religious, private, and public. The forensic remains a key concept in that witnessing and testimony are concerned with past events, providing a particular kind of evidence for violation. Although information gathering uses many kinds of evidence (newspaper reports, regulations, photographs, statistics, and medical records), witnessing and testifying either augment records or supply a memory and human perspective for two purposes: activating an audience and thus diminishing the force of oppression. Thus, witnessing and testifying routinely help to shape deliberation and forward-looking policies. The responses of the audience with verdicts and policies, as well as substantive interventions, may be as important as the truth of the violation. Not unlike Cassandra, harmed parties and witnesses need responses as much as an accurate story. Arguments over the fictive and rhetorical nature of memory, witnessing, and testifying abound, suggesting a wavering line between fact and event (Caruth, Felman and Laub, Gilmore). Even so, for an audience to become engaged and perhaps enraged, they need to find the witness's story credible. Yet bystanders' responses may range from indifference, complicity, and crass opportunism to protection, and support (Wiesel, McPhail "Complicity," McPhail "Politics," Mathison et al., Stiehm, Alcoff, Spelman).

As symbolic acts concerned with engaging the forces of oppression, witnessing and testifying have a particular place in speaking back to power, in creating counter-discourses, which denormalize dominant discourses and offer alternative worldviews. The work of a witness such as Charles Bowden is to present the atrocities of Juarez in contrast to the coffee culture of U.S. morning news. In suggesting the U.S. drug culture has the unseen effect of murder in Mexico, Bowden speaks back to the comfortable assumptions of America. Kay Schaeffer and Sidonie Smith conceive the work of rights claims, these acts of remembering and testifying, as issuing "an ethical call to listeners both within and beyond the national borders to recognize the disjunction between the values espoused by the community and the actual practices that occur" (3). If U.S. citizens know of mass murders at the border and do not respond, the witness has called into question our commitment to the rights of others, despite the claims of concerns for the rights of communities in the Middle East and China. Although dependent on memory, witnessing and testify are a particular category of speech act that calls into question daily practices, making them answerable to a culture's espoused values.

While certain types of witnessing and testifying may foreground representing the speaker and her culture—*testimonio* comes to mind—other types are predominantly concerned with representing a particular abuse or injustice and raising a public consciousness and response (Maier and Dulfano, Beverly). What is an appropriate response to representations of suffering? How should an audience be guided to understand the suffering and respond with appropriate action? We hope the essays in this issue will offer direction on these and our earlier questions and initiate conversations concerning evidence, persuasion, and epistemology in human rights rhetoric.

Our contributors' four essays, all of which are critical in orientation, may be divided loosely into historical reclamations of earlier rights talk and contemporary theoretical explorations. In "Human Rights and Civil Rights: The Advocacy and Activism of African-American Women Writers," Jacqueline Jones Royster and Molly Cochran show how nineteenth- and twentieth-century African-American women activists scripted explicit connections between their local projects and the international frameworks of human dignity and rights. In doing so, they constituted U.S. commitments to human rights agenda as well as civil rights. Similarly concerned with the origins of rights representation, Mari Boor Tonn traces the labor work of "Mother" Jones in "'From the Eye of the Soul': Industrial Labor's Mary Harris 'Mother' Jones and the Rhetorics of Display," examining the early use of photos to expand witnessing of exploitation and injustice. Historical and critical studies such as these document the at-times nascent, always temporally unfolding, contingent, and contested struggles to recognize the rights of "Others."

More theoretical and critical in general orientation, the remaining two essays both turn to contemporary public culture and demonstrate the import of how advocates who theorize human rights in discourse, if only tacitly in evident practices. In "Rights Language and HIV Treatment: Universal Care or Population Control?," Cindy Patton considers how the convergences of two incommensurable "rights" rhetorics create different positions of witnessing. In contrast to the three-decades-long approach to HIV rights based in equality of fundamental conditions and the linking of rights empowerment to effective HIV response, a new paradigm of "Seek and Treat" has shifted the base to epidemiology, disease prevention, and population. Though the earlier witnessing illness requires the presence of the people who are ill, witnessing disease observes the epidemic from the perspective of those who are not subject to the disease. Patton demonstrates how the language of witnessing rights can register deep, distorting epistemological and ontological gaps that hide agendas. In a perhaps unanticipated turn, Erik Doxtader's "A Question of Confession's Discovery" examines the scene of transitional justice through the problems that confession poses for the perpetrators, victims, and broader communities. Consideration of witnessing by perpetrators through their confessions, he suggests, can unpack and deepen an underlying question regarding the movement between the confession's re-cognition and recognition in relation to potential discovery. An afterword by Wendy Hesford incisively places the editors' introduction and ensuing four essays in conversation with each other and her own views concerning human rights rhetoric.

References

Alcoff, Linda. "The Problem of Speaking for Others." *Cultural Critique* 20 (Winter 1991–1992): 5–32. Print.

Austin, J. L. *How To Do Things With Words.* (1962) Cambridge, Mass: Harvard University Press, 1975. Print.

Ballengee, Jennifer R. *The Wound and the Witness: The Rhetoric of Torture.* Albany: SUNY Press, 2009. Print.

Beverly, John. *Testimonio: On the Politics of Truth.* Minneapolis: University of Minnesota Press, 2004. Print.

Bourdieu, Pierre. *Language and Symbolic Power.* Cambridge, Mass: Harvard University Press, 1991. Print.

Brown, Wendy. *Regulating Aversion: Tolerance in the Age of Identity and Empire.* Princeton, NJ: Princeton University Press, 2006. Print.

Burke, Kenneth. "The Rhetoric of Hitler's Battle." *The Philosophy of Literary Form: Studies in Symbolic Action.* Berkeley, CA: University of California Press, 1973. 191–220. Print.

Burke, Kenneth. *A Rhetoric of Motives.* Berkeley: University of California Press, 1969. Print.

Caruth, Cathy. *Unclaimed Experience: Trauma, Narrative, and History.* Baltimore: John Hopkins University Press, 1996. Print.

Cmiel, Kenneth. "The Emergence of Human Rights Politics in the United States." *Journal of American History* 86.3 (December 1999): 1231–1279. Print.

Cmiel, Kenneth. "The Recent History of Human Rights: Review Essay." *American Historical Review* 109.1 (February 2004): 117–135. Print.

Crenshaw, Kimberlé. "Whose Story Is It, Anyway? Feminist and Anti-Racist Appropriations of Anita Hill." *Race-ing Justice, En-gendering Power: Essays on Anita Hill, Clarence Thomas, and the Construction of Social Reality.* Ed. Toni Morrison. New York: Pantheon, 1992. 402–440. Print.

Daly, Mary. *Gyn/Ecology: The Metaethics of Radical Feminism.* Boston: Beacon Press, 1990. Print.

Davis, Ossie. "The English Language is My Enemy." *Language, Communication, and Rhetoric in Black America.* Ed. Arthur Lee Smith. New York: Harper & Row, 1972. 49–57. Print.

Doxtader, Erik. *Faith in the Work of Words: The Beginnings of Reconciliation in South Africa.* East Lansing: Michigan State University Press, 2009. Print.

Dworkin, Andrea. *Letters from a War Zone.* New York: Lawrence Hill, 1993. Print.

Felman, Shoshona and Dori Laub. Ed. *Testimony: Crises of Witnessing in Literature, Psychoanalysis, and History.* New York: Routledge, 1992. Print.

Foster, Francis Smith. *Witnessing Slavery: The Development of Ante-Bellum Slave Narratives.* 2nd ed. Madison: University of Wisconsin Press, 1994. Print.

Gilmore, Leigh. *The Limits of Autobiography: Trauma and Testimony.* Ithaca, NY: Cornell University Press, 2001. Print.

Hasian, Marouf. *Rhetorical Vectors of Memory in National and International Holocaust Trials.* East Lansing: Michigan State University Press, 2006. Print.

———. *In the Name of Necessity: Military Tribunals and the Loss of American Civil Liberties.* Tuscaloosa: University of Alabama Press, 2005. Print.

Hesford, Wendy S. and Wendy Kozol. "Introduction." *Just Advocacy? Women's Human Rights, Transnational Feminisms, and the Politics of Representation.* Eds. Wendy S. Hesford & Wendy Kozol. New Brunswick, NJ: Rutgers University Press, 2005. 1–29. Print.

Hope, Diane S. "Communication and Human Rights: The Symbolic Structures of Racism and Sexism." *Speech Communication in the Twentieth Century.* Ed. Thomas W. Benson. Carbondale: Southern Illinois University Press, 1985. 63–89. Print.

Ignatieff, Michael. "Is the Human Rights Era Ending?" *New York Times.* 5 February 2002. A29. Web. 6 April 2010.

Jamieson, Kathleen Hall. "The Binds that Tie." *Beyond the Double Bind: Women and Leadership.* New York: Oxford University Press, 1995. Print.

Kennedy, David. *The Dark Sides of Virtue: Reassessing International Humanitarianism.* Princeton, NJ: Princeton University Press, 2004. Print.

Kiss, Elizabeth. "Alchemy or Fool's Gold." *Vital Speeches of the Day* 62.24 (Oct. 1, 1996): 755–760. Print.

Maier, Linda S. and Isabel Dulfano, eds. *Woman as Witness: Essays on Testimonial Literature by Latin American Women.* New York: Peter Lang, 2004. Print.

Mathison, Maureen, Mark McPhail, and Mary Strine. "Forum." *Communication Theory* 7.2 (1997): 149–185. Print.

McPhail, Mark. "Complicity: The Politics of Negative Difference." *Howard Journal of Communication.* 3.1–2 (Summer/Fall 1991): 1–13. Print.

———. "The Politics of Complicity: Second Thoughts About the Social Construction of Racial Equality." *Quarterly Journal of Speech* 80.3 (1994): 343–357. Print.

Merry, Sally Engle. *Human Rights and Gender Violence: Translating International Law into Local Justice.* Chicago: University of Chicago Press, 2006.

Mutua, Makau. "Savages, Victims, and Saviors: The Metaphor of Human Rights." *Harvard International Law Journal* 42 (2001): 201–245. Print.

NPR Staff. "Journalist Chronicles 'Killing Fields' of Juarez." Morning Edition 1 April 2010. Web. 6 April 2010. <http://www.npr.org/templates/transcript/transcript.php?storyId=125427225>.

Oxford English Dictionary Online. Oxford University Press. Web. 21 April 2010.

Rich, Adrienne. "The Burning of Paper Instead of Children (1968)." *Collected Early Poems, 1950–1970.* New York: Norton, 1993, 363–366. Print.

Roosevelt, Eleanor D. "The Struggle for Human Rights." *Human Rights and Genocide.* Washington, DC: Department of State, 1949. 1–12.

Ross, Rosetta E. *Witnessing and Testifying: Black Women, Religion, and Civil Rights.* Minneapolis: Fortress Press, 2003. Print.

Schaeffer, Kay and Sidonie Smith. *Human Rights and Narrated Lives: The Ethics of Recognition.* New York: Palgrave, 2004. Print.

Scott, Joan W. "On Experience." *Feminists Theorize the Political.* Eds. Judith Butler & Joan W. Scott. New York: Routledge, 1992. 22–40. Print.

Spelman, Elizabeth. *Fruits of Sorrow: Framing Our Attention to Suffering.* Boston: Beacon, 1997. Print.

Stiehm, Judith Hicks. "The Protected, The Protector, The Defender." *Women's Studies International Forum* 5 (1982): 367–376. Print.

United Nations. "The Universal Declaration of Human Rights." *United Nations Bulletin* 6 (Jan.–June 1949): 6–8. Print.

Whalen, Lucille. *Human Rights: A Reference Handbook.* Santa Barbara, CA: ABC-CLIO, 1989. 199–201. Print.

Wiesel, Elie. "The Perils of Indifference." 12 April 1999. Millennium Lecture Series, East Room of the White House. Web. 6 April 2010. <http://www.historyplace.com/speeches/wiesel.htm>.

Human Rights and Civil Rights: The Advocacy and Activism of African-American Women Writers

Jacqueline Jones Royster & Molly Cochran

Royster and Cochran use the words of African American women writers to enrich our view of intersections between American civil rights discourses and the discourses of human rights as a global concept. They focus on both individual and collective activities of the women and contextualize this activism within the larger framework of the rise of individual human rights language in twentieth century international relations.

> ...in every human Breast, God has implanted a Principle, which we call Love of Freedom; it is impatient of Oppression, and pants for Deliverance, and by the Leave of our Modern Egyptians I will assert, that the same Principle lives in us [enslaved Africans in the United States]. God grant Deliverance in his own way and Time, and get him honor upon all those whose Avarice impels them to countenance and help forward the Calamities of their Fellow Creatures. This I desire not for their Hurt, but to convince them of the strange Absurdity of their Conduct whose Words and Actions are so diametrically opposite.
>
> —Phillis Wheatley, "Letter to Samson Occom,"[1] 11 February 1774

---

[1]Sam Occom (1723–1792), a progenitor of Native-American literature, was a Mohegan minister and political leader who worked to protect the cultures, traditions, and practices of indigenous peoples. He was an advocate for their political autonomy, spiritual well-being, and their education, as evidenced by his associations with Dartmouth College.

This essay disrupts the view that civil rights activism in the United States and human rights activism around the globe occupy different discourse horizons,[2] asserting first that the separated view is an under-interrogated framework, especially when considering that civil rights and human rights are both anchored by notions of human dignity, social justice, social courage, and social action.[3] Further, we assert that an analysis of African American women's writings over time through the intersections of these lenses offers provocative springboards for a more inclusive understanding of this dynamic convergence. Finally, this essay highlights several compounding factors in the twentieth century related to the emergence of human rights within the arena of international relations, noting that, historically, concepts of human rights and human dignity functioned within the specific authority and purview of nation-states, rather than as a universal concept, and underscoring that over the twentieth century there was a transformation in this operational pattern that has given greater visibility at the level of national and international governance to the notion that all human beings have natural rights that transcend national boundaries. This change, in turn, has made more visible the longstanding, under-acknowledged linkages between civil rights discourses within the United States and human rights discourses around the globe.[4]

At this convergence of human and civil rights, the work of African-American women writer/activists becomes instructive. Civil rights discourses as discourses that have been shaped within the authority and purview of the United States as a nation state, in effect, have cast the notion of civil rights as "human" rights in shadow, rather than within the scope of civil/human rights as a coherent and rightful universal concept. By contrast, African-American women writers, as specific exemplars of civil rights rhetoric in the United States, have persistently linked the two, indicating in their writings an abiding ideological commitment to the idea that all human beings, regardless of personal identity or geographical location, are endowed with the dignity of being human and innately deserving of rights by virtue of being human. Thus, when we examine civil and human rights through the eyes of African-American women writer/activists, we see, first of all, a

[2]A simplistic measure of this positioning is a keyword search of a top-ranked research university's library (The Ohio State University). "African Americans Civil Rights" yielded 1,346 entries. "African Americans Human Rights" yielded 194 entries.

[3]For a complementary argument about connections between civil rights and human rights, see Kirt Wilson's Keynote Address at the 2010 Public Address Conference on Human Rights, "More than Civil Rights: The Fight for Black Freedom as a Human Rights Struggle." Also, as noted below we are distinguishing between human rights as a set of values, policies, and practices exercised by individuals and groups and human rights values, policies, and practices that function universally in international relations and thereby beyond the boundaries of nation-states.

[4]In presenting this analytical framework, we note the persistent ways in which the master narrative of self-determination, peace, and justice for all gave rise to special allowances among the Western powers, creating various illogicalities for those not in power, a situation that, as we explain with more detail below, has pushed persistently the double-edged sword of hope and rage/despair.

history of resistance to any compartmentalization of civil and human rights, but secondly we also notice that their claims and arguments offer a compelling rationale for this separation of horizons to be more robustly interrogated as a sociopolitical construction.[5]

An Illusion of Difference

Inside the shell of the national mythos of the United States (our deeply seated systems of cultural memory and belief), civil rights discourses are viscerally and inexorably linked to American slavery as a United States institution that was defined by the legal labeling of human beings as chattel or "non-human" beings without status and without human or civil rights. This racist and ethnocentric framing of African Americans as "non-humans" existed historically in conjunction with the discomforting framings of others who are similarly colored by issues of race, language, culture, caste and class, including, for example, the servitude of indentured whites, the genocide of indigenous communities across North America, the discriminatory treatment of various peoples who have migrated across our southern, western, and eastern borders, and the imperialist occupation by the United States of various territories, for example the Hawaiian Islands (1898–the present), the Philippine Islands (1899–1946), and Haiti (1915–1934). Within the shell of "nation," all of these mythological imperfections have been comparably mis-aligned with motifs of the United States as the land of the free and the home of the brave. Their realities do not match the master narrative of freedom, truth, and justice.

Certainly, provocative discourses about freedom, justice, and equality have emerged and flourished for centuries via this set of discontinuities and interrelationships and continue dynamically within contemporary arenas. However, historically, such arguments within the context of the United States as a nation, rather than as an international leader of nations, have not gained a presence in human rights discourses with a capacity to affect significantly heroic master narratives or motifs related to the moral leadership and socially conscious service of the United States to the world. Within the shell, the nation has challenges; outside of the shell, it is persistently positioned, and positions itself, as an advocate for and protector of the rights of others around the globe, despite these internal challenges. In other words, as Phillis Wheatley suggests (1774) in the opening epigraph, over the full history of our nation, internal discourses about human rights have occupied disconcerting and strangely absurd sidebars in opposition to national policies and practices.[6]

---

[5]The analytical framework for this essay is drawn from Royster's larger manuscript project, currently entitled *A Nation Within: Utopian Desire, Radical Action, and the Voices of African American Women.*

[6]In addition to its linkages with Christian discourses, Wheatley's quotation also suggests the impact of Enlightenment values on human rights discourses and a more inclusive approach to human dignity and human rights. Further, a case can be made that Wheatley positions herself as a witness to this "absurdity," the discontinuity between the words and actions that prevailed so dramatically during her era.

Historically, instead of linking civil rights discourses and activism at home with the avowal of human dignity and human rights around the globe, American civil rights are mapped in the national imaginary as "peculiar" (Stampp, 3), much like the institution of slavery itself to which such interests have been affectively linked.[7] In affective rather than cognitive constructions, these discourses are positioned inside the United States as annoying, as an inconvenient and unfortunate weakness in our national rationale. In effect, affective constructions relate justice, fairness, and equity at lower levels of generality to issues of race, caste, culture, language, class, and later gender, than at more abstract levels of generality with regard to human dignity, human rights, and the pursuit of human possibilities. Consequently, when the specter of discontinuities arises between policies and practices at home and policies and practices abroad, typically, they are quite immediately re-cast in their affect, not as human rights issues, but as curious and vexing mis-alignments within an otherwise normal national landscape.

As vexing peculiarities, the operational expectation for civil rights discourses is that they should quite necessarily be over shadowed by more reasonable and realistic claims for national attention, in light especially of the national motif of the United States being the champion of truth, liberty, and justice—except, perhaps, when enactments of civil rights activism spill over chaotically and cannot be ignored as in times of crisis: a civil war, organized uprisings for sovereignty or social justice, boycotts for fair and equitable treatment, the aftermath of the Hurricane Katrina disaster, and so on. In turn, these spillovers need to be treated affectively as "surprises" to be contained, "handled," re-cast in manageable terms. As surprises, spillovers can be set aside as innocuously as possible within the national purview, as abnormal and not in the interest of human rights at home. Attention is re-directed to acknowledging annoying imperfection while sustaining national image and authority.

Given this type of affective contextual framing, the effort to take civil rights discourses more seriously as rightly and reasonably connected to human rights as a universal value brings to bolder relief within the national shell our most deeply seated taboos—principally, the messy and often unspeakable problematics of race, caste, class, gender, language, religion, culture, and so on, the very elements that have shaped and defined American civil rights discourses. Often, these discourses function as difficult, if not impossible dialogues that make those who look too closely at them or speak too directly about them appear vulnerable to labels of extremism, scarred and blinded by the effects of peculiarity and abnormality, and subject to feelings of guilt, rage, and despair. This process of mythic circumcision, persistently positioning civil rights with a wariness, excises civil rights within the discourse arena as symbolically profane and "untouchable." Civil rights activism, as an internal rather than a universalizing discourse, becomes an aberration that we would have

[7] For a book-length treatment of affective mapping, see Flately.

go graciously unnoticed, so that we might focus instead on images and definitions that stand with propriety in the heroic terms of the nation state as the land of the free and home of the brave, with the mythos of a free and just society safe, secure, and still largely undisturbed by these peculiar, peripheral critiques.

This affective positioning indicates that, while civil rights has been an amazingly vibrant arena of research, scholarship, writing, and activism for more than the two hundred plus years of our national existence, this arena remains essentially unto itself, as a "museum piece"[8] surrounded ultimately by silences and veils. William E.B. Dubois articulated this positioning in 1903 as the "problem of the color line," as life "beyond the veil." In 1944, Gunnar Myrdal called it "an American dilemma." In 1984, bell hooks linked it to the sociopolitical dynamics of margin-center relationships. Since then, many contemporary scholars, such as Kirt Wilson, continue to point out interconnections between the discourses of American civil rights activism and human rights. Arguably, however, despite such efforts, there remains a deeply seated tendency to keep these discourses in separated categories, with civil rights considered to be distinct from and peripheral to human rights debates, focused on the consequences of a peculiar history within the national arena and occupying, as it were, a different conceptual space—as a sidebar or an afterthought.[9]

African-American Women Activists and the Concept of Human Dignity

> As I study present day problems and touch them, I am more and more convinced that we need just such an organization as you are fostering [the International Council of Women of the Darker Races] ... If we are to be a part of the world's program and find favor for our needs we must also learn to share our little.
>
> —Addie Hunton, Vice President of the International Council of Women of the Darker Races, in a letter to Margaret Murray Washington, President 1924. (Hoytt, 55)

The social activism of African-American women functions boldly amid the "peculiar" discursive context of American civil rights. The continuities of oppression experienced by this group have been well documented over the last three decades.

[8]This use of "museum piece" mirrors the use of this term by Spitzack and Carter (407).

[9]Insightful and compelling as a discursive framework, the quest for "civil rights" as a response to the disempowering conditions and effects of slavery, rather than the quest for "human rights" as a global concept, has been the norm in scholarly analyses of racial oppression in the United States. Examples of civil rights scholarship include leading scholars, such as: Stampp; Woodward; Gutman; Franklin; Sundquist; and others. More attention to the connection of struggles in the United States for civil rights to struggles globally for human rights include: Eric Foner; Anderson; Henry J. Richardson, III; Shuler; Soohoo, Albisa, and Davis; and others.

As rhetors, they have been passionate advocates for freedom, social justice, and sociopolitical change—speaking out courageously as witnesses to oppression; inventing organizational structures and using systems, processes, and resources strategically and creatively to define, enable, manage, and sustain change; maximizing opportunities; creating legacies of possibility. While their advocacy has been anchored by their lives and conditions within the United States, they have proclaimed, nevertheless, intricate connections between their status and needs and the larger human enterprise. Instead of linking their resistance to their own racial identity or even to the combination of their race, class, and gender identities as a challenge to national authority, they persistently have defined themselves by their humanity, their human dignity, and their rights to justice, equality, and empowerment within the human enterprise.

So, what does it mean to assert that African-American women have had a global vision of their social activism, have connected themselves in a politically and socially conscious way with the plight of others, and served as steadfast witnesses to oppression as a global concept? What does it mean to claim that their advocacy of civil rights has been consistently linked to human rights, rather than just to a questioning of agency and authority in American race relations? As suggested by the preceding discussion, it is to say that African-American women writer/activists have drawn on the idea of and language of *human dignity* to make social justice for all of humanity, including themselves, a priority. In underscoring this connection between human dignity and social justice, we bring to bolder relief the extent to which these writer/activists function well beyond the more simplistic terms of their drawing strength from religious beliefs to bear witness against oppression. This connection between civil and human rights makes clearer that, in addition to whatever spiritual grounding may be evident in their actions, these writers also have used this conceptual linkage to go beyond spirituality and Christian morality to establish, as well, traditions of social, economic, and political critique.

First of all, by necessity, with the positioning of African Americans as "non-human" chattel, African-American women activists were not simply required in their acts of persuasion to demand civil rights because of the general "degraded" status of their race or their lack of agency and authority in a racist and ethnocentric society. They were quite literally called on to engage in the already larger project of reclaiming, after centuries of oppression and abuse, their own humanity and the potential of that humanity, an activist project that continues into the twenty-first century, for example, through the participation of African-American women in the work of transnational feminisms.[10] Historically, however,

[10]Space limitations do not permit a full explanation of how transnational feminist scholarship (e.g., Alexander and Mohanty) has enriched contemporary human rights discourses or how women of African descent, including African-American women writers, continue to be pacesetters in making insightful connections, analyses, and interpretations.

by their resolve or their personal tenacity, the very first order of business was to claim and proclaim the right to be human and to be treated humanely in social, economic, political, and cultural contexts. Consider, for example, the statement by Maria Stewart in her first published essay, "Religion and the Pure Principles of Morality, The Sure Foundation on Which We Must Build":

> All the nations of the earth are crying out for liberty and equality. Away, away with tyranny and oppression! . . . Many think, because your skins are tinged with a sable hue, that you are an inferior race of being, but God does not consider you as such. He hath formed and fashioned you in his own glorious image, and hath bestowed upon you reason and strong powers of intellect . . . and according to the Constitution of these United States, he has made all men free and equal. (29)

Stewart did not separate racist oppression in the United States from her sense of what should be appropriate for human beings. Instead, she offered testimony, a rationale for its place within the scope of "all the nations of the earth" who were "crying out for liberty and equality." She connected her sense of natural law (i.e., the hand of God) with human dignity and human rights, but also with the U.S. Constitution, making the connection that slavery is un-natural and inhumane by "divine" decree, but also un-lawful.

African-American women advocated for their race (and themselves as the women of that race) to be treated with respect as socially and ethically responsible human beings with a full range of human potentialities, including their desires to function as intellectual beings with agency and authority over their own lives but also as rightful citizens of the nation and the world. Being socially and ethically conscious, however, they did not limit their visions of possibilities to themselves and their own "degraded" group in the United States, or limit the obligations to advocate for social justice to themselves either. They extended this conceptual framing to articulate social and ethical responsibilities as inclusive of all. For example, Frances Ellen Watkins Harper, the most well-known African-American woman creative writer of her day, delivered a speech entitled "Woman's Political Future" in 1893 at the World's Congress of Representative Women. The convention was held from 15–22 May in Chicago at the Columbian Exposition during "The Civil and Political Status of Women" session. Harper stated:

> Let the hearts of the women of the world respond to the song of the herald angels of peace on earth and good will to men. Let them throb as one heart unified by the grand and holy purpose of uplifting the human race, and humanity will breathe freer, and the world grow brighter. (Logan *With Pen*, 46)

While Harper sustained the anchoring of her ideological positioning in Christian motifs, she amplified the connections between human dignity, peace, and justice to the existence of "human" as the quintessential qualifier for "race," and human rights as the cornerstone for national and global happiness.

The linkage between human dignity and social activism helps us see that the greatest hopes and expectations of African-American women writer/activists during this era were not simply to achieve freedom and social justice through their civil rights activism but to write themselves onto the human landscape. In pushing for full membership as human beings within human societies with human rights, they raised for themselves and everyone the notion that the rights of human-ness are innate, and that this factor carries with it social and ethical obligations, not just for African Americans but for all. In basic ways, they honored the maxim to "do unto others as you would have them to do unto you" as a bedrock principle, not for the existence of human rights, but for the exercise of human rights in full measure—which they positioned as the global enterprise for all of humanity, an enterprise that is not controllable by the vagaries of nations. By their testimony, being human equals acting humanely toward all, regardless of status, condition, place, or peoples.

Consider also Ida B. Wells-Barnett who articulated a similar view. Wells-Barnett was a world renowned journalist and crusader against lynching, which she articulated within the terms of both civil and human rights as savage and unlawful acts of terrorism. In a speech delivered at Tremont Temple on 13 February 1893, she railed against the Republican Party, the party of Abraham Lincoln. In her view, they were not fulfilling their commitment to champion human liberty and human rights as the law of the land. She harkened back instead to an earlier generation of outspoken national leaders who actually stood up for their beliefs in humanity and human rights, unlike the Republicans of her era who remained silent in the face of terrorism even as leaders with the authority and ethical obligation to do otherwise. Wells stated:

> I long with all the intensity of my soul for the Garrison, Douglas[s], Sumner, W[h]ittier and Phillips who shall rouse this nation to a demand that from Greenland's icy mountains to the coral reefs of the Southern seas, mob rule shall be put down and equal and exact justice be accorded to every citizen of whatever race, who finds a home within the borders of the land of the free and the home of the brave. (Logan *With Pen*, 98–99)

Wells-Barnett was a champion of human rights as the rights of citizenship. Her core argument was that there was a disconnect between the national belief in America as the land of the free and the home of the brave and national policy and practice, which permitted mob rule against its citizens to go uncontested.

If the persistence of African-American women activists in framing civil rights as rooted in human dignity and human rights were all of the story of their ideological linkages between these two discourses, then it would be a meaningful story. However, these individual connections are not all. There is also a story of collective international action. Consider two examples of the ways this group extended the scope of connectivity beyond national boundaries and crafted, not just as a bare-boned and disembodied ideological claim to freedom and justice, but individual and collective commitments to global human rights.

A prime example is the activist work of "race woman" Mary Church Terrell, a founder and the first president of the National Association of Colored Women (NACW), founded in 1896 as the first cohesive national network of African American women to address social and political issues. Terrell was an affluent, well educated, well traveled, multi-lingual woman who was well versed in international affairs. Her experiences in connecting American civil rights and global human rights constitute a striking example of the direct and active participation of African-American women in both discourses through collective action, and their deepening understanding of the need to declare, by both their cognitive and affective insights, the importance of social justice as a global concept. In her autobiography, *A Colored Woman in a White World*, Terrell discussed several moments of her participation and leadership, among them the two moments chronicled below.

In 1904, Terrell was invited to deliver two addresses at the International Congress of Women on 13 June in Berlin, Germany. As the only woman of African descent invited to speak, she reported feeling the weight of representing both African-American women and the whole continent of Africa. She described presenting one speech fluently in German and a second one fluently in French, and indicated how affirmed she felt that she was able to place the problems and issues of women of African descent within the purview of such an esteemed international group of women in languages that they knew and could understand better than English (Terrell, 197–208). In other words, Terrell offered persuasive testimony about the global expanse of the human landscape—connecting herself to histories of oppression, the desire for freedom and justice, and the right to human agency and authority.

In another instance, Terrell explains that in 1918, after World War I, her alliance with the Peace Movement was growing. She narrates how she received a letter from the Woman's Peace Party, a section of the International Committee of Women for Permanent Peace, inviting her to be one of the American delegates to the Women's International Congress on Peace and Freedom which was held in Switzerland, in April of 1919, five months after the armistice was signed. As Terrell explains, the American delegation selected her to speak to the convention on their behalf. However, she also wished to present a resolution protesting the "discrimination, humiliation and injustices perpetrated, not only upon the colored people of the United States, but upon the dark races all over the world" (333). The resolution caused considerable controversy among the delegation but, ultimately, after various attempts to thwart Terrell's efforts, she was permitted to read the following resolution:

> We believe no human being should be deprived of an education, prevented from earning a living, debarred from any legitimate pursuit in which he wishes to engage or be subjected to humiliations of various kinds on account of race, color or creed. (333)

That same evening, Terrell presented her address fluently in German, as one of only six speakers. She made several points related to the focus of the meeting. However, as she sought to do in the resolution, Terrell also proclaimed that:

> A lasting peace is impossible as long as the colored peoples [races] are subjected to injustice simply because they are colored, and as long as they are prevented from learning and being trained in any of the activities leading to the pinnacle of human aspirations and for which they possess the natural ability, energy and dedication. (Women's International League of Peace and Freedom, 213–214)

In her discussion of this distinctive moment, Terrell explained how gratified she was to be chosen to speak on behalf of the American delegation and their commitments to world peace, but she also explained how painfully aware she was that:

> There was not a single delegate from Japan, China, India or from any other country whose inhabitants were not white. For the second time in my life it was my privilege to represent, not only the colored women of the United States, but the whole continent of Africa as well . . . it finally dawned upon me that I was representing the women of all the non-white countries of the world. (Terrell 331–2)

Terrell was aware that her voice represented African Americans and served as witness for millions of absent others. While Terrell did not emphasize directly that her ability to participate in these gatherings was enhanced by the fact that she was a "white-skinned" African-American woman, she did explain directly that the Europeans generally did not recognize that she was a "colored" woman and that in her speeches she was determined to make her racial identity clear to all. By all accounts, Terrell did bear witness in this international context "for the darker races" and did so quite eloquently.

A second example of the global reach of African-American women writer/activists emerges from their own organization of the short-lived International Council of Women of the Darker Races—as indicated in the quotation at the beginning of this section from Addie Hunton. In a document dated 10 November 1924, Margaret Murray Washington, president of the NACW from 1914–1918 and spouse of Booker T. Washington, records the formation of the group as four years before in 1920.[11] She reports on the first public meeting in Chicago at the Bethesda Baptist Church, stating that the organization grew out of the vision and desires of leaders in NACW with the purpose of:

> . . . the dissemination of knowledge of peoples of color the world over, in order that there may be a larger appreciation of their history and accomplishments and so that they themselves may have a greater degree of race

[11]This explanation is based on Eleanor Hinton Hoytt.

> pride for their own achievements and touch a greater pride in themselves. (Hoytt, 54)

Washington also reported that in attendance were NACW members and two young women students from India; that there were written or oral reports on conditions in Haiti, Cuba, the Virgin Islands, and West Africa; and that the group committed to two specific actions: "forming of Committees of Seven everywhere" and "securing of a closer cooperation and understanding between colored and white women in this country" (Hoytt, 54). The research of Eleanor Hoytt confirms that the Committees of Seven did indeed organize study groups, recommend readings, and promote the reading of African-American texts in the public schools, and express concern about understanding the conditions and status of women and children in West Africa, Haiti, Cuba, and India—going on field trips to various countries and engaging in philanthropic activities in support of international education projects (55).[12]

A closer examination of the history of African-American women's participation in civil rights discourses over time confirms that they made their own contributions to what we understand by human dignity and the importance of making human rights the subject, not only of American justice, but international justice with discrimination toward none. However, to acknowledge this participation properly and to ground their contributions both historically and theoretically, it is important to have at least a general sense of linkages between human rights and international politics in the twentieth century. Although a thorough accounting of this history is beyond the scope of this brief essay, the section that follows acknowledges a few critical points.

Establishing Human Dignity and Human Rights as a Global Value

> ... they [the United States of America and the United Kingdom] respect the right of all peoples to choose the form of government under which they will live; and they wish to see sovereign rights and self-government restored to those who have been forcibly deprived of them ...
>
> —President Franklin D. Roosevelt and Prime Minister Winston Churchill, "The Atlantic Charter," 14 August 1941

[12]Note that elite African-American women broadened their horizons in the twentieth century through foreign travel, with increasing numbers participating in both individual and organized trips. By the mid-twentieth century, foreign travel had become a booming business among this group, as evidenced by the highly successful Henderson Travel Agency, founded in 1955 by African-American woman entrepreneur Freddye Henderson in Atlanta, Georgia. Furthermore, the push to be philanthropic was very much in motion, as verified by Gill's discussion of the community activism of beauticians in *Beauty Shop Politics: African American Women's Activism in the Beauty Industry* (2009).

Statements like the one above, made only months before the entry of the United States into World War II, underscored two competing points. First, in the practice of international relations in the early twentieth century, rights discourses in international arenas did not pay much heed to the rights of individuals. Only states, not individuals, had personality in international law. The diplomacy of this period lacked an actual discourse of individual, rather than collective, human rights. The welfare of individuals—if thought about at all—was understood to be best realized in the protective shell of the sovereign state. Universal human rights in international relations discourse did not surface in a substantial way until the mid-twentieth century via the emergence of the Peace Movement and the League of Nations; the joint declaration of the Atlantic Charter by Great Britain and the United States; the formation of the United Nations in 1945; and most dramatically with the passing of the United Nations Declaration of Human Rights.

In essence, after the ending of World War I, liberal internationalists, concerned that no war like World War I should ever happen again, encouraged the building of an international institution to ensure lasting peace, the League of Nations, which formed in 1919 with its first council meeting taking place in 1920. While ultimately the League failed, the effort enabled critical expressions and the development of a discourse that linked the welfare of individuals with the possibility of world peace. Writers such as John Dewey and J. H. Tufts argued, for example, that the value of social institutions at any level—sub-national, national and international—is whether they "equalize opportunity for all" and develop our capacities as human beings (431). Dewey saw the League of Nations to be a failure in this respect, however, because it was a forum of governments alone, not peoples, and those governments were still in possession of their sovereign right to declare war.

Others participants in the discourse, inspired by similar principles connecting peace and social justice, viewed the League to be a starting point, however flawed, and tried to influence the shape of the new international organization through advocacy. One such attempt was made by the Women's International League of Peace and Freedom (WILPF). Interestingly, through the work of transnational, non-state organizations, and new forms of diplomacy conducted through the channels of newly minted international organizations (such as the International Labor Organization established in 1919 through the Treaty of Versailles) and the League of Nations (1919–1920), human injustices began to receive some redress at the international level. Agents such as these gave rise to the creation of international societies with connections across national boundaries. Because these organizations were not governmental organizations, the imperatives of state interests were either absent or modified, and they were able to cajole action from states and to encourage cooperation between states in areas where there had never been cooperation before.

In other words, nongovernmental international organizations exercised influence on issues of international politics that directly impacted the welfare of individuals and their human dignity. Examples include: the coordination of humanitarian assistance to relieve food shortages both during and immediately after World War I; the raising of matters of self-determination as represented in treaties reached after World War I; the intervening of the League of Nations in the election in the Saar region of Germany to ensure the democratic autonomy of individuals in the region; and the developing of recourses against discrimination, authorizing individual petitions to the Mandates Commission for dependent territories within the League of Nations. These actions are important in themselves for work they did towards reinforcing a concept of human dignity. Still, there was no language of human rights to concretize a commitment to the justice of individuals in international practice. Individual human rights were still held as the purview of nation-states (including the United States) to attend, manage, and monitor—or not.

The formation of the League of Nations brought the advent of a formal international organization composed of nation-states which not only paid lip service to the connection of peace and security with social justice issues, but created a committee, the Sixth Committee on Social Questions, to bring these concerns under the purview of the Secretariat and its work. Even so, human rights work was not seen to be the REAL work of the League. The Covenant of the League had no explicit human rights language, a gap that was due principally to a stand-off between Japan and the American and British delegations. These delegations were working aggressively to avoid a racial equality clause that the Japanese wanted. Having such a clause, however, was terribly worrisome for the United States, given its legacy of slavery and racial discrimination, and for the British, given their worldwide colonial enterprises. Furthermore, at the end of the day, the League of Nations did fail, and in the 1930s another World War was rising. Despite this basic failure, however, the League succeeded in furthering the cause of human dignity and human rights, as suggested, for example, by World War II being popularly identified as the war "to make the world safe for democracy"—for freedom, truth, justice, human dignity.

By fits and starts, the spirit of commitment to human dignity and human rights steadily gained traction across the twentieth century with the advocacy of many individuals and groups in Western countries,[13] but also with the activism and hard work of many more in non-Western countries worldwide. By mid-twentieth century the ground began to shift and nation-states were prepared to build the discourses of human rights in a more robust way. This conceptual framework came to be employed more regularly in international diplomacy, and more organizations were founded to articulate, advocate for, and protect human rights (e.g., WILPF and the International Council of Women of the Darker Races). One

[13]For example, prominent writer H. G. Wells drafted an international bill of rights in his *New World Order.*

such advocate was Franklin Delano Roosevelt, who was elected U.S. president in 1932 when the League was beginning to decline.

Roosevelt was a firm believer in the connection between international peace and security and the welfare of humanity, as evidenced by his 1941 State of the Union Address. There he argued that aggression grows out of human deprivation and persecution and named the four freedoms:

> . . . we look forward to a world founded upon four essential human freedoms . . . freedom of speech and expression—everywhere in the world . . . freedom of every person to worship God in his own way . . . freedom from want, which, translated into world terms, means economic understandings which will secure to every nation a healthy peacetime life for its inhabitants . . . freedom from fear, which, translated into world terms, means a world-wide reduction of armaments to such a point . . . that no nation will be in a position to commit an act of physical aggression against any neighbor—anywhere in the world.

After World War II, Roosevelt was a key player in the formation of the United Nations, the new organization that would take up the cause of peace and security started by the League of Nations.

One of the first commissions to be established at the United Nations was the Commission on Human Rights. First Lady Eleanor Roosevelt, a human rights activist in her own stead, was named Chair. Using the concept of "Four Freedoms," she and the drafting subcommittee navigated well the complex challenges of articulating a "universal" vision of human dignity and human rights and crafted an international bill of rights.[14] Interestingly, the Universal Declaration of Human Rights (GA Res 217 [III] of 10 Dec 1948) was not a legally binding document. It was presented instead as a moral argument (similar to the positioning of the more recently crafted Declaration on the Rights of Indigenous Peoples, adopted by General Assembly Resolution 61/295 on 13 September 2007). Even with the covenant being more morally than legally binding, the language of the declaration provided, nonetheless, a normative guidepost against which human rights movements continue to hold nations to international public account (Glendon). The Declaration proclaimed human dignity as a primary value in international law,[15] with Article 1 stating: "All human beings are born free and equal in dignity and rights. They are endowed with reason and conscience and should act towards one another in a spirit of brotherhood" (UNDHR, United Nations). Further, the Declaration

[14]The drafting subcommittee was composed of eight individuals from the United States, Lebanon, Great Britain, France, China, Australia, Chile, and the U.S.S.R., which appointed a "working group" of the first four state representatives listed. Rene Cassin, the lead author in drafting the UDHR, states all 58 nations contributed to the final shape of the UDHR. The UDHR was adopted unanimously, albeit with eight abstentions from the Eastern bloc, on 10 December 1948.

[15]Dorothy Jones discusses why the positioning of the term dignity in the Preamble and Article 1 is significant as a statement of intent for the whole document.

puts on a firmer footing a principle that was nascent during the era of the League of Nations, that is, that "Everyone is entitled to all the rights and freedoms set forth in this Declaration, without distinction of any kind ..." (UNDHR, Article 2).

Most striking in the Declaration is that it also laid out economic, social, and cultural rights in addition to civil and political rights, emphasizing, for example, rights to work; equal pay for equal work; a right to rest and leisure; a wage adequate to provide for one's health and well-being, including food, shelter, and medical care; a right to education; the right to participate in the cultural life of the community; all of which are declared in Article 22 as an entitlement, "indispensible for his dignity and the free development of his personality" (UNDHR, United Nations). This slate of declarations offers a compelling and more inclusive framework for interpreting the longstanding concerns of American civil rights discourses as human rights discourses and for the activism of African-American women writer/activists in them.

Re-Invigorating the Intersections Among Civil and Human Rights Discourses

As the discourses of human dignity and human rights gathered momentum by mid-twentieth century, so too did struggles for civil rights inside the United States. In the first half of the twentieth century, African Americans fought for democracy abroad—twice—and supported the war efforts at home. When World War II ended, given its spirit of freedom, truth, and justice, African Americans wanted, indeed expected (as they had expected after the American Revolutionary War) to see that their sacrifices had not been in vain, that there was indeed democracy abroad and at home as well—for them as a people, who had been enslaved, dominated, and oppressed in every aspect of their lives. Keeping the world safe for democracy necessarily suggests that change—at home—would have to come. They were disappointed. Their world—inside the authority and purview of the United States—had not changed. It was the same as it had been for generations. Civil rights activism escalated in the twentieth century and evolved by mid-century into the Modern Civil Rights Movement, suggesting that African Americans felt ever more deeply the difference between the mythos of universal human rights globally and their own lack of rights and agency—at home.

While there is not space in a short essay to chronicle the long and substantial history of the American Civil Rights Movement as simultaneously a movement for freedom, justice, and equality *and* for human dignity and human rights, sampling the texts of African-American women continues to offer a mechanism by which to post milestones for critical engagement. After more than two centuries of individual and collective action, African-American women writer/activists remained outspoken about civil and human rights as a grand landscape. Consider one last example from the late twentieth century, drawn from June Jordan's 1985 essay collection *On Call: Political Essays*. Recognized for both her inclusiveness and her radicalism, Jordan used both her poetry and her prose to provide sharp-tongued critiques of a full range of political issues related to the involvement (or lack of involvement) of the U.S. government in complex international issues. She was particularly impatient with what struck her as an underlying lack of connection between the avowed values and beliefs of the United States and our actions and inactions both in the United States and around the world. In "Moving Beyond the Enemy: Nicaragua and South Africa," she stated:

> In Nicaragua, the people want to defend the democratic sovereignty that they fought for. In South Africa, the people want to defend themselves from the atrocity of apartheid and to achieve the sovereignty that universal human rights confer. Perhaps the most important contribution we can make to international justice is just this: Stop United States' collaboration with the enemies of self-determination. This will keep us busy. This will run us ragged. This may make the difference that so many millions of First World peoples live for: The difference between freedom and death. (145)

Here Jordan sees her plight and that of others in the United States as inextricably connected to human rights as a global concept. As the title of her collection suggests, Jordan places the United States and all of its people, including herself, on call. Moreover, she insists that we are obligated to uphold these principles and act on them deliberately and consistently—regardless of the site of crisis. In doing so, Jordan joins a long line of African-American women writer/activists who have linked their own futures to the future of all human beings and who have linked, as well, their own social obligations for action to the global human enterprise. African-American women writers and activists have consistently proclaimed, as documented in this analysis, that they see themselves by all of their personal and group identities in the company of others as human beings who are endowed with the dignity of being human and innately deserving of universal human rights.

References

Alexander, M. Jacqui and Mohanty Chandra Talpade, eds. *Feminist Genealogies, Colonial Legacies, Democratic Futures.* New York: Routledge, 1997. Print.

Anderson, Carol. *Eyes off the Prize: The United Nations and the African American Struggle for Human Rights, 1944–1955.* New York: Cambridge University Press, 2003. Print.

"Atlantic Charter." The Avalon Project. Yale Law School. Lillian Goldman Law Library. 14 August 1941. Web. 25 October 2010.

Dewey, John, and J. H. Tufts. *Ethics* (1908) in *The Middle Works 1899–1924, John Dewey, The Collected Works,* InteLex Corporation 5: 431. Print.

DuBois, William E. B. *The Souls of Black Folk.* 1903. New York: Gramercy Books, 1994. Print.

Flately, Jonathan. *Affective Mapping.* Cambridge: Harvard University Press, 2009. Print.

Foner, Eric. *The Story of American Freedom.* New York: W. W. Norton, 1998. Print.

Franklin, John Hope. *From Slavery to Freedom: A History of Negro Americans.* Fifth Edition. New York: Alfred A. Knopf, 1980. Print.

Gill, Tiffany M. *Beauty Shop Politics: African American Women's Activism in the Beauty Industry.* Urbana: University of Illinois Press, 2010. Print.
Glendon, Mary Ann. "Knowing the Universal Declaration of Human Rights." *Notre Dame Law Review*, 73.5 (1998): 1153–1190. Print.
Gutman, Herbert G. *The Black Family in Slavery and Freedom, 1750–1925.* New York: Vintage/ Random House, 1976. Print.
hooks, bell. *Feminist Theory: From Margin to Center.* Cambridge, MA: South End, 1984. Print.
Hoytt, Eleanor Hinton. "International Council of Women of the Darker Races: Historical Notes." *SAGE: A Scholarly Journal on Black Women*, V.III.2 (Fall 1986): 54–55. Print.
Jones, Dorothy. "The Declaratory Tradition in Modern International Law." *Traditions of International Ethics.* Eds. Terry Nardin and David R. Mapel. Cambridge Studies in International Relations. V.O. Cambridge: Cambridge University Press, 1992. 42–61. Print.
Jordan, June. *On Call: Political Essays.* Boston: South End, 1985. Print.
Logan, Shirley Wilson. *With Pen and Voice: A Critical Anthology of Nineteenth-Century African Women.* Carbondale: Southern Illinois University Press, 1995. Print.
Myrdal, Gunnar. *An American Dilemma: The Negro Problem and Modern Democracy.* New York: Harper & Brothers, 1944. Print.
Richardson, Henry J., III. *The Origins of African-American Interests in International Law.* Durham: Carolina Academic Press, 2008. Print.
Roosevelt, Franklin Delano. "The Four Freedoms." *American Rhetoric.com.* 6 January 1941. Web. 8 November 2010.
Shuler, Jack. *Calling Out Liberty: The Stono Slave Rebellion and the Universal Struggle for Human Rights.* Jackson: University of Mississippi Press, 2009. Print.
Soohoo, Cynthia, Catherine Albisa, and Martha F. Davis, eds. *Bringing Human Rights Home: A History of Human Rights in the United States.* Philadelphia: University of Pennsylvania Press, 2009. Print.
Spitzack, Carole and Kathryn Carter. "Women in Communication Studies: A Typology for Revision." *Quarterly Journal of Speech* 73.4 (November 1987): 401–423. Print.
Stampp, Kenneth. *The Peculiar Institution: Slavery in the Ante-Bellum South.* 1956. New York: Alfred A. Knopf, 1967. Print.
Stewart, Maria W. "Religion and the Pure Principles of Morality, the Sure Foundation on Which We Must Build." *America's First Black Woman Political Writer.* Ed. Marilyn Richardson. Bloomington: Indiana UP, 1987. 28–42. Print.
Stewart, Maria W. "Religion, and the Pure Principles of Morality, The Sure Foundation on Which We Must Build." 1831. *Maria W. Stewart, Americas's First Black Woman Political Writer.* Ed. Marilyn Richardson. Bloomington: Indiana University Press, 1987. 28–42. Print.
Sundquist, Eric J. *To Wake the Nations: Race in the Making of American Literature.* Cambridge: Harvard University Press, 1993. Print.
Terrell, Mary Church. *A Colored Woman in a White World.* 1940. Salem, New Hampshire: Ayer, 1986. Print.
United Nations Declaration on the Rights of Indigenous Peoples. United Nations. 13 September 2007. 2 November 2010.
The Universal Declaration of Human Rights. United Nations. 10 December 1948. Web. 17 October 2010.
Wells, H. G. *New World Order.* London: Martin Secker and Arburg, 1940. Print.
Wheatley, Phillis. "Letter to Samson Occom (1774)." *The Prentice Hall Anthology of African American Women's Literature.* Ed. Valerie Lee. Upper Saddle River, NJ: Pearson/Prentice Hall, 2006. 4–5. Print.

Wilson, Kirt. "More than Civil Rights: The Fight for Black Freedom as a Human Rights Struggle." 12th Biennial Public Address Conference. Human Rights Rhetoric: Controversies, Conundrums, and Community Actions. University of Pittsburgh. 30 September http://xrl.us/wilsonkeynote. Web. 30 October 2010.

Women's International League for Peace and Freedom. University Library, Special Collections. University of Illinois at Chicago. Web. 9 November 2010.

Woodward, C. Vann. *The Strange Career of Jim Crow.* Third Edition. New York: Oxford University Press, 1974.

"From the Eye to the Soul": Industrial Labor's Mary Harris "Mother" Jones and the Rhetorics of Display

Mari Boor Tonn

Mary Harris "Mother" Jones was among the U.S. industrial labor movement's savviest practitioners of visual politics to champion human rights for workers. This article focuses on two key features of Jones's exploitation of the power of "the eye" for persuasive ends: first, was her keen appreciation of the rhetorical potency of the camera as an emerging technology with differing force for varied audiences, and second, was her trademark spectacles ritualizing rebellion, showcasing workers' resolve, and generating publicity. To mine these visual features, this essay situates them within two significant historical episodes: the Colorado Coalfield War of 1913–14, especially the Ludlow Massacre, and the Children's Marches of 1903 she led to lobby for child labor reforms.

If the early U.S. labor movement compiled a trilogy of industrial infamy, events of April 20, 1914, in a temporary strikers' tent colony outside of Ludlow, Colorado, would surely count among it.[1] Then and there, enemies of unionism's increasing political muscle ignited a literal and metaphoric firestorm set within one of the bloodiest protracted altercations between U.S. capital and labor—the Colorado Coalfield War of 1913–1914. Shoring up the 14-month-long stand-off's notoriety was its title as the most photographed labor conflict in the nation's coal mining history. Over months, photographers—ranging from coal company employees, photojournalists, amateur passersby, and professional free-lancers—chronicled in hundreds of images a sobering slice of lower working-class life in

[1]This essay was presented first at the Biennial Public Address Conference on Human Rights Rhetoric hosted by the University of Pittsburgh, 30 September–2 October 2010. A webcast of the original presentation may be found at http://xrl.us/boortonn. The author thanks Lester Olson for the opportunity to present this research and respondents and reviewers—Lester Olson, Cara Finnegan, Lawrence Prelli, Arabella Lyon, Mari Lee Mifsud, and Wendy Hesford—who have enriched it.

isolated coal communities largely invisible to a citizenry daily comforted by coal (Margolis). Searing pictures preceding and surrounding April 20, its explosive aftermath, and industry propaganda campaigns to contain the damage, added to a growing visual album underscoring the power of images and spectacle in early U.S. labor challenges to common industrial practices inimical to contemporary conceptions of human rights.

Among the first U.S. social movements to exploit myriad forms of rhetorical display in championing human rights protections,[2] industrial labor contributed to expanding, elevating, and accelerating consideration of human rights to a global imperative unfolding following World War I and eventually codified in the 1948 United Nations' "Universal Declaration on Human Rights" (UDHR).[3] Resembling a utopian fantasy penned by workers in mines and factories redressing lived experiences bordering on industrial slavery, the UDHR censured servitude of any kind, arbitrary arrest, detention, or exile; professed allegiance to freedom of expression, liberties to pursue ownership of personal property, and access to legal tribunals to adjudicate criminal charges; it also cataloged the following rights to be ascribed at birth: favorable work conditions, leisure born of reasonable limitations of work hours, education, and freedom to join a union for self interest and protection. Resonating in the UDHR is profound concern for the individual even as it underscores collective responsibility and power.

The journey of the U.S industrial labor movement to the Declaration and beyond is an epic tale—its obstacles monumental, its methods diverse, and its consequences profound. Thus, this essay confines exploration of this movement's human rights crusade to its concerted use of visual politics in the service of social justice. Specifically, I focus on one principal figure—an elderly white-haired widow and the movement's most charismatic and effective union agitator, Mary Harris "Mother" Jones—and two pivotal national events: the Colorado Coalfield War, especially Ludlow, and the earlier 1903 marches of textile mill children led by Jones to lobby for federal child labor reforms. Extraordinary as Jones was, I treat her as what Kenneth Burke would term "a representative anecdote" (*Grammar* 59–61) to excavate the rhetorical ocular in the industrial labor movement to mobilize constituencies, resist oppression, court public sympathy, and refigure national identity and the conception of human rights. I focus on two key features of Jones's

[2]For example, Borda's analysis of women's suffrage parades and substantial review of literature regarding the parade notes that female factory workers in 1860 were the first U.S. social reformers to appropriate the hallowed Revolutionary-era parade ritual for subversive ends (note 2, 49). Abolitionists also occasionally employed sketches of conditions related to slavery, and some engaged in protests one might term theatrical. Revolutionary colonists rebelling against Britain also engaged in various forms of rhetorical display, including the performative and visual, see Olson, *Emblems* and Olson, *Benjamin.*

[3]Given the UDHR was issued shortly after World War II and the Holocaust, its lack of engaging with issues adequately with race and ethnicity is troubling. For concision, I focus on the UDHR as a way to note the obvious ways that labor conflicts seemed to influence it.

"showing forth": first, her keen appreciation of the potency of the camera as an emerging technology perceived as unalloyed "truth" to varied audiences, and, second, her trademark spectacles ritualizing rebellion, showcasing resolve, and generating publicity. Despite the overlap of her employment of photographic images and theatrical display to engage with witness or "the eye," I focus on the episodes of the Colorado Coalfield War and the "Children's Marches," respectively, to contextualize, highlight, and analyze her rhetorical use of visual resources and strategies to realize her goal of securing protections for the disadvantaged and exploited.

I begin first with the 1913–1914 Colorado conflict to situate the visual and performative power and legacy of Ludlow, segue into Mother Jones's biographical baptism into ocular epistemology, and then analyze her use of photography in her public appearances. I then turn to her signature "pageants of poverty" (Fetherling 8), focusing on among the most widely publicized of her countless spectacles—the children's marches of 1903—originating in the Philadelphia textile strike.

The Colorado Coalfield War and Ludlow

Amid September snow and rain in 1913, roughly 200,000 mining family members had migrated to a dozen improvised canvas outposts dotting the Colorado landscape since their immediate eviction from company-issued hovels for holding firm in bargaining with Colorado Fuel and Iron (CFI) and its principal owners: the John D. Rockefeller oil tycoons and the nation's wealthiest family.[4] At the time, Colorado presided as the deadliest U.S. state for coal miners, doubling fatalities in a nation where average deaths tripled Europe's most hazardous coalfields. Even so, Colorado miners' demands privileged autonomy and sustenance over safety: wages for required unpaid "dead work" such as laying track, an elected check man to verify dug coal weights, elimination of pay deductions for coal impurities, and a long-delayed wage hike for tonnage mined. Grievances also included, ironically, insistence that bosses follow existing Colorado laws outlining maximum work hours and stipulating cash wages rather than "scrip" or coupons redeemable only for wildly inflated company housing, supplies, and services. But most irreconcilable was management's refusal to recognize a union with collective clout to police management practice.

Beyond battling hunger and an exceptionally unforgiving Colorado winter, roughly 1,200 striking mining family members huddled in 200 tents outside Ludlow, the largest of the improvised ghettos, for seven months had endured a smorgasbord of political intimidations: daily search-light and machine-gun surveillance, coiled barbed wire dumped in drinking wells, a roaming "Death

[4]Accounts of Ludlow and the Colorado Coalfield War are numerous. For just two, see Fetherling 109–140 and Gorn 199–225. A more exhaustive account is in McGovern and Guttridge.

Special" machine-gun armored car, random sniper fire, frequent beatings, suspension of both habeas corpus and civil courts, which enabled capricious mass jailings, and a saber-slashing cavalry assault injuring several women protesting the first of two lengthy illegal incarcerations in nearby Trinidad of the then 83-year-old Mother Jones (Fetherling 118–121; Gorn 199–214).

On the morning of April 20, Colorado state militia and deputized coal company hirelings began spraying the Ludlow campsite with machine gun fire, triggering a day-long pitched battle with rifle-bearing strikers. Hours into the melee, a lieutenant, who was fond of calling himself and his band of horsebacked soldiers "Jesus Christs who must be obeyed" (Beshoar 124), replied to the plea by the colony's leader to negotiate a ceasefire by first bludgeoning him unconscious, executing him and his truce-seeking comrades, and then displaying their bullet-riddled corpses as warnings for challenging capital's supremacy: a class version of lynching.

Around twilight, militia launched their final assault ("Audience" 1, 7). Soaking tents in kerosene, which Rockefeller Sr. called the "poor man's light" that helped build his massive fortune (*The Rockefellers*), they torched them and looted the colony's humble treasures. When dawn broke, Ludlow families canvassing the smoking ruins for remnants of their threadbare lives amid armed soldiers unearthed another grisly price of their rebellion: In one bunker previously dug underneath tents as havens from periodic flying lead lay the corpses of two pregnant women and eleven children, several just a few months old.

Coined "The Ludlow Massacre" by the United Mineworkers of America (UMWA), the carnage proved incendiary. For ten days, outraged citizens joined vengeful strikers along a 40-mile corridor in a battle with militia and coal-company hirelings, which was finally quelled by the arrival of federal troops. When the strike limped to its end in December, violence had claimed scores of lives with exponentially more wounded, still but a sliver of several hundred annual Colorado mining casualties.

The Colorado Coalfield War has spawned numerous writings, in part, I argue, because of the multitude of photographs recording for all to "see" the various fingers of gilded-age industry's iron fist. To compare, two months into the Colorado walkout, a false cry of fire by anti-union stewards in a crowded union hall on Christmas Eve during the copper miners' strike in Calumet, Michigan—where the dozens trampled to death in the ensuing stampede included 62 children—generated fewer pictures and, thus, far less ink (Fetherling 141). Similarly, in feudal-like West Virginia, wee-hour assassinations of sleeping union sympathizers in their Paint Creek coal-company shacks in 1903 or the unparalleled bombing by government squadrons on its own citizens during the 1921 Blair Mountain strike largely escaped the camera's eye and public notice (Fetherling 35, 188). But Colorado resonated. Photographs of hardscrabble shanties, grinning militia manning machine guns, torched ruins of Ludlow and the demolished Forbes colony, the "Death Pit" (http://wwwa.du.edu/ludlow/index.html), and funeral processions honoring Ludlow's slain were among the vast warehouse of speaking images from which contending parties drew in order to grapple with armed class warfare and to tame feared class revolution exploding shortly across the globe. Colorado coalfield photographs animated special Congressional Hearings convened on mining conditions, further inflamed labor papers, and punctuated the public talk of Mother Jones throughout the remainder of her life. The frozen stills of brute industrial peonage also thawed apathy of the mainstream press and public as few, if any, U.S. class conflicts had before or since. *The New York Times*, for example, compared Ludlow victims to "trapped rats" and termed the incident "a story of horror unparalleled in the history of industrial warfare" (*The Rockefellers*).

Public outcry over Ludlow, in turn, prompted a Rockefeller media blitz to rehabilitate the Rockefeller image, earning Standard Oil consultant Ivy Lee (whose portfolio later would include Germany's Third Reich) stature as the alleged father of public relations.[5] Particularly astute was John D. Rockefeller, Jr.'s autumn journey to Colorado coalfields from where reports and images of the financier chatting with coal miners, holding their children, and dancing with their wives generated headlines. The Rockefeller family's machinations momentarily charmed even the crusty Mother Jones, whose multiple unlawful imprisonments and deportations from the state ironically had been engineered by coal industry clout. Criticized as gullible by labor comrades, Jones defended her uncharacteristic mercy toward the Standard Oil heir by invoking witnessing as route to social truth or "theoria," a term originating in literal sight. Mere months following the Colorado strikers' concession, she remarked: "Rockefeller [Jr.] is part of a system that he was born to—that he can't help. Only by going down into Colorado for himself, by *seeing* the thing . . . can he help [the workers] . . . I think Rockefeller wants to do the right thing, but he's *blind.* How can he *see*?" (Barnes 100–101, emphasis added).[6]

Jones's expressed faith here in the ocular and experiential as key to nourishing moral action reflects both her tortured history of witnessing imperiled bodies and her fifty-year crusade in making the nation "see" class injustice. Born into poverty and revolt in Ireland sometime in the 1830s, a young Mary Harris experienced her grandfather hung for insurrection, witnessed soldiers destroy her home seeking her insurgent father, and gazed on British militia with heads of Irish rebels impaled on bayonets. In her later U.S. years, she watched her husband and four children perish from yellow fever and then looked on as her home, livelihood, and possessions turned to ashes in Chicago's Great Fire.[7] Witnessing thus birthed her trust in truths midwifed by literal sight, impelled her fearless courting of

[5]Heath and Combs focus primarily on Lee 48–55, but Gorn also discusses the key role of William Lyon Mackenzie King, hired as an expert on labor (220–222).

[6]Barnes's interview with Mother Jones occurred on 7 February 1915, two months after the Colorado strike ended.

[7]Various biographical accounts exist of Mary Harris Jones's hazy early years. See Fetherling 3, Gorn 7–46; Mother Jones's autobiography contains few sentences on her life before joining labor's cause.

martyrdom, and helped position her as early labor's savviest practitioner of rhetorical display—the visual, ritualistic, and theatrical.

Legendary as the early labor movement's most spellbinding orator, Mother Jones nonetheless regarded the "eye" as most forceful in conveying the anguish of industrial slavery necessary for its amelioration. "[S]cribbling, " she once said, "has no effect on the public mind. If you *show*... real evil and wake up the sleepy, indifferent public, you will get these conditions changed" (Steel *Speeches* 250, emphasis added). Her trust in witness—literal or supplied by theatrics or the camera's magic—as eclipsing the ear as the pathway to knowledge resonates in her hauntingly poetic reply to a reporter's query in Ludlow's wake about what had prompted her crusade:

> That is the question that forty million other fools before you have asked.... I was born of the struggle and the torment and the pain. A child of the wheel, a brat of the cogs, a woman of the dust, for even iron has its dust...
>
> And so how can you ask, and how can I tell you when I began to care? You ask because very probably none of you *know*—you haven't *seen* our lives as we live them out there in Colorado. We can tell you, and you can listen, but no tragedy was ever comprehended that went from the mouth to the ear. It has to pass from the *eye* to the soul. (Barnes 97–98, emphasis added)

Although Jones's visual theatrics indicted capitalists for varied crimes and lobbied for labor reforms, their undergirth always was epideictic, which others have exalted as a chief rhetorical mode resonating with ethical human impulses informing debates in pragmatic public forums. Jeffrey Walker claims epideictic display shapes social codes and reflects the deep value commitments by which communities live and identify themselves. Epideictic, he claims, may both reinforce and transform conventional beliefs (1–9). Similarly, Lawrence W. Rosenfield points to epideictic as fostering necessary contemplation on human beings as "Being" (137) in fundamental joys, duty, or love. Epideictic, he argues, "persists as the form most reliant on the meditative faculties of mind" and, thus, distinctly capable of "reach[ing] to the core of all political life" (150). As both suggest, epideictic may cast audiences not simply as spectators in the Aristotlean sense but also as ethical actors given that moral display may influence individual "civic conduct" (Prelli 4). To be sure, visual display of codes and identities are not uniformly moral, benign, nor always persuasive as evident in ritualized lynchings and attendant visual practices. Still, one antidote to visuality in the service of social perversion is a counter showing forth.

Mother Jones and the Camera

Despite advancing age, outdated matronly attire, and ascetic lifestyle, Mother Jones was no Luddite, early on embracing the camera as a potent developing technology capable of refuting denial of industrial conditions and piercing social conscience. Cumbersome photographic modes in use since around her birth occasionally had provided shadowy glimpses into lower-working class life (Davenport 45), but revolutionary photographic advancements in the 1880s coincided roughly with Jones's first estimated labor actions, among them her apprenticeship with the flamboyant populist Jacob Coxey in his 1894 publicity march of unemployed to the nation's capitol to lobby for government work projects (Gorn 62–63). By then, the Progressive Era had ushered in overtly politicized documentary photojournalism, illustrated by Jacob Riis's 1890 exposé, *How the Other Half Lives*, recording the bleak underbelly of working-class life in New York City tenements (Twigg; Davenport 94). By 1900, introduction of the dollar Brownie camera meant increasingly less could escape the lens, including occasional glimpses of open class warfare in godforsaken coal camps where miners, who rarely saw the color of their children's eyes in sunlight and sometimes worked seven days a week under constant watch of armed guards, teetered on the precipice of starvation.

A nomad frequently operating in stealth under dangerous conditions, Mother Jones left an incomplete trail of her visual prowess. Reporters sometimes accompanying her in wading frigid creeks under cloak of darkness to evade arrest typically fixed on the broader dimensions of her mesmerizing appeal for the workers she empowered. Even existing full transcripts of her public statements, including Congressional testimony, honed in on transcribing her fiery words with stenographers noting that she exhibited photographs. Still, extant remains of her correspondence and public talk testify to her robust appreciation of pictures in exposing what she termed "horrors [which] cannot be depicted by the human pen" (Steel, *Speeches*, 201), a view later captured in Lewis Hines's oft-quoted claim, "If I could tell the story [of child labor] in words, I would not need to lug around a camera." For her part, Jones viewed photographs as means to terrify labor adversaries, mobilize workers, and engage the public with class injustice. In one surviving letter, for example, a comrade reports mailing her photographs and searching for others (Steel *Correspondence* 317). Preceding her signature parades, she sometimes schooled marchers on how to comport themselves advantageously before the camera, and her common orders in public talks to "put [that] down, Mr. Newspaper man" sometimes included photographic stage directions. Jones's reminders to workers of anti-labor stewards' fear of the camera as evidentiary proof is illustrated in a repeated tale of a reporter jailed simply for interviewing her. "It was the most amusing thing you ever saw," she said. "Hollis had a [K]odak [when] they arrested him. [The] two armed guards . . . . held it like it was a bomb" (Foner 197). Rockefeller, Jr. himself repeatedly recoiled from Ludlow images during Congressional hearings, even putting his hands in front of his face to avoid seeing the grainy snapshot submitted by a mother of the laid-out corpse of her young son slain there while comforting his terrified young sister ("Rockefeller Again").

Given the inexactitude of historical records, the precise images Mother Jones occasionally exhibited in her speeches remain captive to speculation. Yet clues provided in her recorded talk guide my treatment of how such visual tokens functioned rhetorically in her hands to puncture public indifference, challenge adversaries, and mobilize and empower her labor constituency.

For neutral and skeptical audiences, photographs of industrial malfeasance worked in multiple ways. Images of machine guns, corpses, and charred ruins of daily life helped foster for audiences living in relative comfort what Burke calls a new "perspective by incongruity," wherein symbolic clash shatters previous orientations, thereby opening space for fresh outlooks (Burke *Attitudes* 308–311). Illustrative of visuality's fracturing force is Christine Harold and Kevin Michael DeLuca's argument that "the dialogue between photos" of the young black Emmitt Till's mutilated body and his smiling Christmas snapshots on his casket intensified revulsion of his lynching and catalyzed civil rights rebellion (275). Lawrence Prelli similarly claims the statue of African-American Arthur Ashe amid Confederate heroes on Richmond, Virginia's famed Monument Avenue is "jarringly incongruous with the embodied Confederate story" (14). And Davi Johnson concludes, echoing Burke, of explosive Birmingham images in 1963 that "[p]hotographs can be epiphanic, forcing a psychic transformation of the citizenry by rupturing imagined conceptions of identity" (8). Black and white images, indeed, often proved exactly that, drawing in starkest relief the gulf between alleged moral conviction and common praxis, thereby erasing alleged gray areas to which moderates sometimes safely clung.

Much like Burke's notion of deliberate misfits creating perspective by incongruity, Mother Jones sometimes explicitly employed visual juxtaposition to shatter cemented social premises servicing class oppression. During Congressional hearings three days after Ludlow, she answered pressing questions about merits of free enterprise and open shops by couching her proposal for government ownership of mines in the epideictic virtue of communal obligation which she then underscored via filmed stark contrasts:

> [I]t is the duty of every man and woman who has consideration for the people of the nation—just to see how much money those fellows made in 1912, and see the starving wretches . . . . [Exhibiting some pictures.] Now, here is picture of the tents. Here is a picture of the home of the millionaire. Here is a picture of the money [the industrialists] made in one year alone. (Foner 395)

Immediately positioning photographs of workers exiled to makeshift cloth homes in frozen wilderness against the top-hatted and silver-caned opulence of Rockefeller industrial royalty—whose estate was five times the acreage of Monaco (*The Rockefellers*)—turned, in mere seconds, the Protestant work ethic's hallowed promise of prosperity for industriousness inside out. Notable in her major premise ("It is the duty of every man and woman who has consideration for the people of this nation to . . . see") is the implicit expectation that true, moral citizens will follow a logic of shortened premises supplied by the eye, a trust evident in the bald simplicity of her captioned talk—"Here is a picture of the tents. Here is a picture of the home of the millionaire." Grounded in epideictic community values of care and obligation and through the rhetorical topos of contrast, she invites audiences as active witnesses to complete their own forensic and deliberative conclusions. Relying here upon the vocabulary of witness, Jones "bluntly compress[ed] a compelling narrative" (Johnson 6) of class injustice meriting political remedy.

Certain enduring Colorado Coalfield War photographs also illustrate what Roland Barthes calls the "*punctum*" of an image, a "prick, sting, a speck, a cut, a little hole," an "element that arises from a scene, shoots out like an arrow, and pierces.... A photograph's punctum is that... which pricks me (but also bruises, is poignant to me)" (Barthes 26–27). Unlike what he terms the banal "*studium*" of many staged photographs eliciting a distanced "like/dislike" response to the picture's artistic or even political intentions or merits, for example, an image's punctum engages the viewer through a personal emotional response of tenderness or "loving" (27). Images from Ludlow that appear on various labor websites nearly a century later suggest the forceful subjective pathos of punctum. Pictures of iron bedsprings or crooked kitchen stoves stoically resisting Ludlow's blaze potentially sting and move by inviting an enthymematic imagining of a "before" in the image's recorded "after" (Figure 1). As Barthes writes, "the *punctum*... is a kind of subtle *beyond*—as if the image launched desire beyond what it permits us to see.... [P]unctum has, more or less, a power of expansion.... Punctum is... what the reader adds to a photograph...." (45). Indeed, photographs of charred Ludlow ruins totally absent of human life necessarily tap personal experiences of the viewer, conjuring haunting poignant ghosts of meals cooked and shared and

Figure 1 Stove.

the comforting relief of bedtime and the warmth of its intimate encounters. The emotive potency of many photographs, Barthes suggests, "deriv[es] from a kind of second sight, which . . . may carry [us] back to somewhere in [ourselves]" (40). The "prick" here in a photo of deliberate destruction is not unlike the compelling exhibit in the U.S. Holocaust Museum—the piles and piles of wrinkled shoes requiring visitors to paint in the lives of the lost persons who once wore them.

So, too, the photograph of a lone slumped figure facing the camera amid Ludlow rubble potentially lacerates viewers, as witnesses, on multiple levels (Figure 2). The man's posture suggests soulful weariness amplified by a blank expression reflecting the incomprehensible weight of his surroundings. Yet his position in the near left of the image's frame with the ruins stretching behind him also enable a hopeful reading of trudging-through and also forward despite the horrors at his back. Beyond recording evil inhumanity, the photograph's unstaged humanness likewise aids healing by its subtle reminder of the curative of care. To walk among the indescribable filth and stench of smoldering ruins and rotting flesh, this shell-shocked man has chosen to keep his jacket, white shirt, and hat in a eulogistic gesture of tenderness or "loving" for a community destroyed.

Jones also employed photographs as a potent counter-argument during charged encounters with labor enemies, converting public spaces into courtrooms where she presided as prosecutor and judge and oscillated between casting various audience members as jurors and defendants. In a 1920 public meeting heavily

Figure 2 Figure at Ludlow.

infiltrated by hissing coal company operatives, she countered open hostilities with rapid fire damning photographic evidence mirroring the literal weaponry in images she displayed:

> I want you to see this. (Exhibiting a photograph.) Do you see it? It is rapid firing gun, a machine gun.... Here is another one (Exhibiting another picture.)... There is the funeral of the fifteen babes that they murdered in Ludlow, Colorado. I have the pictures. Here are some more of the dead [who] were murdered by those machine guns. Here is some more of them.... Here, I want to show you. Here [are] Baldwin-Felts men that left West Virginia and went to Colorado and [local authorities] put the State uniform on them... Look at that (showing another picture) This is the blood of the babes that stained the mountain. (Steel *Speeches* 226, 228)

Again, by juxtaposing images of machine guns and uniformed soldiers, funerals of infants, and corpses set against burnt skeletons of communal life in visual enumeration, Jones ruptured possible presumptions that such battles were fair moral fights. Such photographs, accompanied by her defiant pronouncement—"I have the pictures"—functioned in an era of faith in photographic technological realism akin to contemporary faith in DNA. Much of photography's magic, Susan Sontag reminds, is an image's ethos as "something directly stenciled off the real" (Sontag 154). In this adversarial labor encounter punctuated by images of bloodshed and sneering dismissal of it, Barthes claim of photography's coercive force is amplified by irony. "The photograph is violent: not because it shows violent things," he writes, "but because... *it fills the sight by force* [;]... in it nothing can be refused or transformed...." (91). Still, Jones's forensic showing-forth did not end with only those crimes captured by the lens; rather, her surrounding talk of other class violence renders such photographs as what Cara Finnegan terms "visual synecdoches": images "representative of a[n] [oppressive] system," or "one interlude in a larger drama" (*Picturing* 87).

Varied meanings of photographs, of course, develop in a darkroom of interplay with other texts. Jones's withering indictments of class violence through pictures were embedded within detailed narratives of collective guilt, extending to public apathy and workers' own complicit poor judgment and cowardice. Her passing sentence via graphic images she further animated in words demanded all viewers—oppressors, oppressed, and the indifferent—contemplate and judge themselves. Her talk surrounding the photographs she displayed amplified their power as what Bruce Gronbeck terms "hailing devices" to spur the exercise of viewers' individual agency true to personal sense of self (xxii). As Sontag writes, "Photographs cannot create a moral position, but they can reinforce one and can help build a nascent one" (17).

At the same time, for constantly beleaguered lower-class workers, especially rural coal mining families living among the farthest removes from social notice and concern, the pictures Mother Jones displayed potentially functioned in far-reaching ways. In an era before Kinko's, PowerPoint and ubiquitous big screens, to assume that most persons in audiences of sometimes thousands even could see from distant perches the photographs she exhibited would be naive. Nonetheless, her dramatic waving of photographs, coupled with continual reminders of their existence—"*I have the pictures*"—offered a psychic empowering balm by bearing tangible witness to their workers' lived experiences. As Barthes states, "[I]n photography I can never deny that the thing has been there . . . . (76)" and "Every photograph is a certificate of presence" (87). Sontag concurs, noting that photographs are a "way of certifying experience," and a "defense against anxiety," "help[ing] people take possession of a space in which they are insecure" (9). Bitter fruits of oppression, after all, are not simply material, brutal as they sometimes prove to be. The tentacles of oppression also wind their way into the victim's psyche, instilling fear, worthlessness, and despair, fortified by public denial or cavalier dismissal. As Finnegan claims in her study of commissioned Depression-era photographs of the unemployed and poor, certain pictures elevated the subject's status, thereby troubling social privilege. Drawing on Sontag's claims that "to photograph is to confer importance," thus making photography a "tool of power," Finnegan argues certain portraits of working poor conferred on them a seldom offered dignity and respect. Finnegan buttresses her claim with Graham Clark's argument that Dorothea Lang's portraiture "inist[ed] upon the 'significance and stature' of her subjects, 'if for no other reason that the *fact* of [their] existence, and the emotional resonance of [their] condition'" (Finnegan *Picturing* 103). In similar fashion, photographs of mining families lined before humble homes, engaged in daily chores and recreation, threatened and killed, and marching with stoic dignity to honoring martyred comrades not only weaved a human narrative with affective power to nudge a nation but also provided a modicum of psychic relief to workers by writing their lives onto the public page. "A photograph not only is like its subject," Sontag writes, "but [is] a[n] homage to its subject" (Sontag 155).

To be sure, images of brutal violence viewed by the oppressed or oppressors can cut various ways—furthering paralyzing terror, normalizing violence, or, conversely, igniting and fortifying rebellion. Whereas some whites historically had used lynching images to celebrate perceptions of superiority, as Harold and DeLuca argue, pictures of Till's lynched body "consumed" and shared by African Americans akin to the Eucharist steeled their resistance (275–278). This practice was a forerunner to the use of postcards bought in the thousands by embattled Belfast citizens in 1974 capturing Irish Troubles they witnessed daily (Sontag 200). So, too, Jews still purchase souvenirs containing Holocaust images as sacred memorials, markers of identity, and totems to ward off that horror's recurrence. In somewhat similar fashion, workers employed photographs of labor's most willing martyr—Mother Jones herself—as talismans to conjure hope, comfort, and courage against formidable odds. Replicating use of religious iconography, some miners adorned their shanty walls with pictures of labor's Mother of Sorrows

(Gorn 118) and pinned her face to their lapels during protest marches, echoing practices of resistant peoples' use of Our Lady of Guadalupe, including during the Mexican Revolution where "Madre" Jones reigned as their living saint of class struggle.

Mother Jones and Spectacle

Beyond photographs, Mother Jones used parades, street theater, and other visual performances in her repertoire of human sights to champion human rights, methods long used by labor. Some 800 striking female shoe factory workers in 1860, for example, had been the first social rebels to appropriate the epideictic Revolutionary-spawned parade to exert cultural presence, call politicians into account, demand reforms, challenge policies, and expose hypocrisy of national ideals. For her part, Jones's trademark "pageants of poverty" included marches—sometimes in the several thousands—of children accompanied by marching bands, parades of workers who sometimes crowned her as labor's "queen," and mop-and-broom brigades of ferocious mining wives armed only with clanging pots and pans, red pepper, hat pins, and wailing babies who petrified scabs, spooked mine mules, shamed timid husbands and sons, and perplexed weary jailers who often released the unruly, singing mothers and their howling broods (Fetherling 41; Gorn 76). Explicitly borrowing photographic language, Jones remarked that an army of resolute women with toddlers in tow makes "a wonderfully spectacular picture" (Gorn 83). Jones's frequent theatrics came to concern even UMWA leadership who worried they siphoned attention from specifics of contract disputes (Fetherling 142), but the notorious maverick nonetheless ignored directives to desist, aware, as was the later Martin Luther King, Jr., that theatrical events helped to focus rather than to divert the public eye, to galvanize public sentiments, not to deflect them. To a reporter just prior to the Colorado strike, she invoked the power of the dramatic, including disruptive cheekiness:

> I have said that I hate violence; I favor drama. We must wake the sleepers somehow, and where blindness can be healed by shock we must provide the shock. Sometimes it hurts a little, but it helps the patient afterward for lo! it makes him see. The Coxey Army's march to Washington was a great joke, but it helped mightily to bring about good roads.
>
> And demonstrations are good things for labor in these learning days. They are good advertising, and the serious, progressive drama as well as comic opera needs advertising. (Foner 510)

Emblematic of what Kevin Deluca calls image event politics and he and Jennifer Peeples describe as "critique through spectacle" (134) were Jones's two marches in 1903 of striking Philadelphia textile workers, including mill children, to lobby for federal child labor regulations, a longstanding cause she convinced skeptical union officials would generate sympathy for the general strike. First showcasing several thousand working children in the City of Brotherly Love, she then fashioned a 125-mile trek of strikers, including 100 children (Foner 438–439),[8] across three states to publicize spiking child labor, which had doubled between 1880 and 1900 to 1.7 million, ironically, in the midst of a cultural shift sacrilizing childhood (Finnegan "Response"). Like other states turning a blind eye to their own child labor laws, Pennsylvania commonly employed children—some as young as seven—who worked 60 hours a week for $2, the lowest salary rung rationalized by mill bosses with the perverse logic that such children had no children to support.

Reportedly inspired by throngs for the Liberty Bell's tour, Mother Jones's "Children's March" featured numerous symbolic nods to colonial rebellion: mill children sometimes dressed as Minute Men, one member swung a red, white, and blue baton, another hoisted an enormous Stars and Stripes, a fife and drum corps played patriotic songs, and the contingent occasionally camped on Revolutionary War battle sites where she delivered rousing speeches comparing class struggles to British tyrannies catalyzing George Washington's earlier rag-tag brigades. Striking youngsters also carried placards mimicking hallowed revolutionary-era sentiments: "WE ASK ONLY FOR JUSTICE," "PROSPERITY: WHERE IS OUR SHARE?," and in echoes of Patrick Henry's defiant cry for liberty or death, "55 HOURS OR NOTHING" (Gorn 131–134). But particularly bruising were banners reminding spectators that occasional theatrical costumes notwithstanding, the marching company of mill children were simply that—mere children and not real soldiers: "WE WANT TIME TO PLAY," and "WE WANT TO GO TO SCHOOL." For onlookers subject to escalating cultural rhetoric romanticizing childhood (Finnegan, "Response"), or with relatively cosseted offspring of their own, frail youngsters bearing placards identifying them as textile workers set against pleadings for common childhood "pursuit[s] of happiness" created incongruities capable of forging new perspectives on standard factory practices.

The longevity of one photograph of Jones's image event again speaks to the unsettling prick of punctum (Figure 3): amid a line of upright rebels dutifully holding signs for the camera is a young boy in the front row crouched with hands on knees and feet turned in and laser eyes as if anticipating a ball somewhere coming into play. Within the photograph's studium of documented rebellion, the boy's unchoreographed movement is the "accident" Barthes describes in rupturing the "unary" of staged photographs or news images whose literalness may "shout" but rarely "wound" (41). Here, the uncontained wiggly energy of youth

[8]In Congressional testimony in 1912, Jones claimed that she organized 6,000–7,000 children for a rally in Philadelphia drawing 50,0000 before taking 75 children on her march to New York. Other reports, however, feature different numbers.

Figure 3 Children's march.

pierces not only because it carries viewers back to a place within themselves but also invites contemplation on this child's adult after: the slow erosion of that endearing spirit viewers glimpse by more years of mundane factory toil. "Photography," Barthes argues, "is subversive not when it frightens, repels, or even stigmatizes, but when it is *pensive*, when it thinks" (38).

Jones's visual stunts critiquing class colonialism were not confined to exploiting 1776 symbols. On the march's eve, she invoked ocular language in forecasting its contours to the press, "I am going to picture capitalism and caricature the money-mad. I am going to show Wall Street the flesh and blood from which it squeezes its wealth" (Gorn 102). And so she did. At Princeton, Jones displayed illiterate, thin, and stooped-shouldered children with gnarled or missing fingers compliments of mill machinery as visual "textbook[s] on economics" to the Ivy League crowd (Jones 76). In practices echoing medieval Carnival detailed by Michael Bakhtin, she also mixed the serious and satirical.[9] Consistent with medieval Saturnalia rituals—which temporarily inverted social relations between rulers and ruled through gross ridicule—Jones employed maneuvers to reverse momentarily social hierarchy in grotesque displays of class privilege, visually converting unbridled pursuits of wealth from the sacred to profane. Along the route, thin, maimed youngsters performed skits lampooning the preening luxuries of "Mr. Capital" and "Mrs. Millowner," augmented with mocking effigies of starched industrial moguls and their heavily encrusted, painted, perfumed, and feathered wives. At Coney Island amid well-heeled vacationers, Jones placed her young

[9]For discussions of Bahktin's notion of the "carnivalesque," see Bahktin, *Rabelais* and Bahktin, *Dialogic*.

rebels in empty zoo cages where they clung to iron bars as visual metaphoric commentary on the beastliness of industrial servitude. There, during her speech before a giant image of Roman emperors with thumbs down while zoo lions roared (Gorn 136), she said in farcical tones: "You see those monkeys in the cages. [Professors] are trying to teach them to talk. The monkeys are too wise, for they fear that then the manufacturers might buy them for slaves in their factories" (Foner 103).

Jones's march also illustrated her hallmark talent for improvisation, which contributed to her unrivalled success in organizing non-English-speaking workers; following the Burkeian notion of "us[ing] all that is there to use" in a particular moment, she would sometimes "speak" to fresh immigrants via bands, record-players, photographs, effigies, visual aids of ousted mining families, and other theatrical displays (Fetherling 178; Gorn 92, 256). During the Children's March when crowds and press attention dwindled, she rejuvenated interest by spontaneously switching its New York City finale to the Oyster Bay retreat of President Theodore Roosevelt, which she publicized by sharing plaintive letters to him with the press. Roosevelt's refusal to grant an audience to her and three exhausted children rendered him what Burke would call the "perfect enemy" (see Burke *Language* 18–19) or foil symbolizing government indifference to industrial malfeasance.

Although Mother Jones's publicity stunt did not immediately usher in child labor reforms she hoped, its theatrics left its mark on the retina of public conscience and identity. The 1903 spectacle paved paths for later child labor campaigns, notably Hine's photographic portfolio commissioned by the National Child Labor Committee, which took the nation by storm in 1916 (Davenport 44). That year, Woodrow Wilson—by then not President of Jones's Princeton stop but of the country—convened recalcritrant Senators to break a stalemate, producing the first federal child labor laws (Cooper 253, 335, 343–344).

Conclusion

The photographs of class warfare and Mother Jones's trademark demonstrations testify to the rhetorical power of images and spectacle employed by the early labor movement, visual precursors to tactics adopted in later social movements. Examining early class struggles further expands the scholarly aperture in considering rhetorical display as potent vehicles to advance human rights. Moreover, detailing specific instances of class conflict—which images inherently force—refocuses treatments of class to lived conditions rather than more abstract theoretical discussions distanced from materiality (e.g., see Schilb 129–130). Mother Jones herself—who helped launch the Socialist Party's most influential newspaper and who was the only female signature on the founding manifesto of the Industrial Workers of the World—often expressed disdain for comrades preoccupied by intellectual class debates, dismissing them as "hot air oratory" and "scribbling" removed from battles in the trenches.

Additionally, the events described here underscore the interplay among class, race, gender, and even age in focusing the public eye. One might reasonably doubt, for example, whether Ludlow would have seared the nation's conscience so intently had its victims been black or what Jones herself sometimes in racist remarks referred to as "heathen Chinese" (Gorn 136). Despite lingering anti-immigration fears, images of tow-headed mill and mining children and embattled European families resonated among the more privileged, in part, by providing a looking-glass through which white onlookers were forced to contemplate their own reflection, albeit in more humble clothes. So, too, Jones's frequent measuring of innocence with the yardstick of age was and is not unique, as illustrated in varied responses to Till's lynching, King's use of marching black youngsters in Birmingham, or the iconic image of an anguished young Vietnamese girl burned naked by napalm (Hariman and Lucaites). But whereas Finnegan argues that the focus on children in Depression-era photographs in popular magazines "infantilized" the impoverished (*Picturing* 198–202), I contend that trumpeting the purity of threatened children may implicitly confer undeserved guilt on severely oppressed adults. Although the gruesome killings of Ludlow mothers and children were horridly unmerited, so, too, was the mowing down of 26 unarmed miners in Lattimer, Pennsylvania, in 1894 and another two dozen in Arnot, Pennsylvania in 1897 (Gorn 77; Fetherling 38), just as was pre-Till random lynchings of grown blacks. merely because they were the handiest targets to exercise white supremacy. Moreover, gender codes exalting motherhood as woman's primary mission not only cushioned criticism of "Mother" Jones's visual militancy but aided in generating public sympathy. Whereas Jennifer Borda argues parading suffragists's "very presence in the streets challenged traditional notions of femininity and . . . restrictions of women's conduct" (26–27), Jones's armies of angry mothers and her frequent parading of children embodied duties fundamental to "womanhood," especially motherhood's fierce protectiveness unencumbered by social rank. As Prelli argues, rhetorical displays of identity convey "what ought and ought not to be" (15), which explains why *The New York Times* claimed the most searing testimony in the fifteen months of Congressional hearings was by one of two young mothers surviving Ludlow's Black Hole describing her frantic, failed efforts to save her three babies first from bullets and then from fire ("Audience" 1, 7).

Yet, despite the camera's power, "photography," Sontag reminds, "inevitably entails a certain patronizing of reality. . . . Cameras miniaturize experiences . . . ." (80, 110). Put differently, photography, as Barthes notes, is a kind of metonymy—a substitution or reduction of life (45). As a 1925 *Report of the U.S. Coal Commission* on coaltowns, most located in West Virginia, stated, "In the worst of the company-controlled communities, the state of disrepair . . . runs beyond the power of verbal description or even photographic illustration, since neither . . . can portray the . . . abandoned dejection or reproduce the smells . . . [the] medley of odors" (quoted in Fetherling 181).

Finally, Mother Jones's rhetorical displays illustrate how epideictic ends—praise and blame, honor and dishonor—need not be either/or but can be both/and. In her hands, the rhetorical ocular honored hallowed motherhood and childhood, worship of work, and sacred revolutionary impulses long defining national identity. But it coincidentally blamed and shamed a people's failures in meeting that very vision of themselves, thereby inviting potential for reform. Using literal witness as lens to basic truths and values fundamental to self-identity as human creatures, Jones melded past, present, and future in images of human suffering, connection, and communal duty impervious to time. In so doing, she—as labor champion—exemplified among the most radical Progressive era efforts to recenter or refigure identity by a nation increasingly reliant upon "the eye" for social truths as it searched anew in looking for its soul.

References

"Audience in Tears as Miner's Wife Tells of Smothering of Three Children." *New York Times* 4 February (1915): 1–7. Print.

Bahktin, Mikhail. *The Dialogic Imagination: Four Essays.* Michael Holquist. Trans. Eds. Caryl Emerson and Michael Holquist. Austin: University of Texas Press, 1981. Print.

———. *Rabelais and His World.* Trans. Hélène Iswolsky. Bloomington: Indiana University Press, 1984. Print.

Barnes, Djuna. *Interviews.* Washington, DC: Sun & Moon Press, 1985. Print.

Barthes, Roland. *Camera Lucida: Reflections on Photography.* Trans. Richard Howard. New York: Hill and Wang, 1981. Print.

Beshoar, Barron B. *Out of the Depths: The Story of John R. Lawson a Labor Leader.* Denver: The Whole World Press, 1942. Print.

Borda, Jennifer L. "The Woman Suffrage Parades of 1910–1913: Possibilities and Limitations of an Early Feminist Strategy." *Western Journal of Communication* 66 (Winter 2002): 25–52. Print.

Burke, Kenneth. *Attitudes Toward History.* Berkeley: University of California Press, 1969. 1984. Print.

———. *Grammar of Motives. 1945.* Berkeley: University of California Press, 1969. Print.

———. *Philosophy of Literary Form.* Berkeley: University of California Press, 1973. Print.

———. *Language as Symbolic Action.* Berkeley: University of California Press, 1966. Print.

Cooper, John Milton, Jr. *Woodrow Wilson.* New York: Alfred A. Knoff, 2009. Print.

Davenport, Alma. *The History of Photography.* Albuquerque: University of New Mexico Press, 1991. Print.

DeLuca, Kevin Michael. *Image Politics: The New Rhetoric of Environmental Activism.* New York: Guilford Press, 1999. Print.

DeLuca, Kevin Michael and Jennifer Peeples. "From Public Sphere to Public Screen: Democracy, Activism, and the Violence of Seattle." *Critical Studies in Media Communication* 19 (2002): 125–151. Print.

Fetherling, Dale. *Mother Jones: The Miners' Angel.* Carbondale: Southern Illinois University Press, 1974. Print.

Finnegan, Cara A. *Picturing Poverty: Print Culture and FSA Photographs.* Washington, DC: Smithsonian Books, 2003. Print.

———. "Response." Public Address Conference, University of Pittsburgh, Pittsburgh, PA. 1 October 2010. <Http://xrl.us/boortonn>. 4 March 2011. Web.

Foner, Phillip S., ed. *Mother Jones Speaks: Collected Speeches & Writings.* New York: Monad Press, 1983. Print.

Gorn, Elliott. *Mother Jones.* New York: Hill and Wang, 2001. Print.

Gronbeck, Bruce E. "Visual Rhetorical Studies: Traces through Time and Space." *Visual Rhetoric: A Reader in Communication and American Culture.* Eds. Lester C. Olson, Cara A. Finnegan & Diane S. Hope. Los Angeles: Sage, 2008: xxi–xxvi. Print.

Hariman, Robert and John Louis Lucaites. "Public Identity and Collective Memory in U.S. Iconic Photography: The Image of 'Accidental Napalm.'" *Critical Studies in Media Communication* 20 (2003): 35–66. Print.

Harold, Christine and Kevin Michael DeLuca. "Behold the Corpse: Violent Images and the Case of Emmett Till." *Rhetoric & Public Affairs* 8 (2005): 263–286. Print.

Heath, Robert Lawrence and W. Timothy Combs. *Today's Public Relations.* New York: Sage, 2005. Print.

Johnson, Davi. "Martin Luther King, Jr.'s 1963 Campaign as Image Event." *Rhetoric & Public Affairs* 10.1 (2007): 1–25. Print.

Jones, Mary Harris. *The Autobiography of Mother Jones.* Ed. Mary Field Parton. 3rd ed. Rev. Chicago: Charles H. Kerr, 1980. Print.

Margolis, Eric. "Mining Photographs: Unearthing the Meanings of Historical Photos." *Radical History Review* 40 (1988): 32–48. Print.

McGovern, George S., and Leonard F. Guttridge. *The Great Coalfield War.* Niwot, CO: University of Colorado Press, 1996. Print.

Olson, Lester C. *Emblems of American Community in the Revolutionary Era: A Study in Rhetorical Iconology.* Washington, DC: Smithsonian Institution Press, 1991. Print.

———. *Benjamin Franklin's Vision of American Community: A Study in Rhetorical Iconology.* Columbia, SC: University of South Carolina Press, 2004. Print.

Prelli, Lawrence J., ed. *Rhetorics of Display.* Columbia: University of South Carolina Press, 2006. Print.

The Rockefellers. Public Broadcasting System, 2006. Television.

"Rockefeller Again Heckled by Walsh." *New York Times* 22 May 1915: 6. Print.

Rosenfield, Lawrence W. "The Practical Celebration of Epideictic." *Rhetoric in Transition.* Ed. Eugene E. White. University Park: The Pennsylvania State University Press, 1984. 131–155. Print.

Schilb, John. "Future Historio-graphies of Rhetoric and the Present Age of Anxiety." *Writing Histories of Rhetoric.* Ed. Victor J. Vitanza. Carbondale: Southern Illinois University Press, 1994. 128–138. Print.

Sontag, Susan. *On Photography.* New York: Anchor Books, 1989. Print.

Steel, Edward M., ed. *The Correspondence of Mother Jones.* Pittsburgh: University of Pittsburgh Press, 1985. Print.

———. *The Speeches and Writings of Mother Jones.* Pittsburgh: University of Pittsburgh Press, 1988. Print.

Twigg, Reginald. "The Performative Dimension of Suveillance: Jacob Riis' *How the Other Half Lives.*" *Text and Performance Quarterly* 12 (1992): 305–328. Print.

Walker, Jeffrey. *Rhetoric and Poetics in Antiquity.* Oxford: Oxford University Press, 2000. Print.

Rights Language and HIV Treatment: Universal Care or Population Control?

Cindy Patton

Over the past three decades, the World Health Organization has negotiated a global consensus among activists, governments, and the pharmaceutical industry with regard to the human rights of persons with AIDS, and those at highest risk of contracting HIV. More recently, epidemiologic modelers have proposed a "treatment as prevention" in which strategies like safe sex and harm reduction are considered unnecessary because mass HIV testing and aggressive maintenance of individual with HIV are believed sufficient to drive down population level viral load, thereby decreasing the individual odds of encounter a person with infectious HIV. This article considers the historical evolution of the human rights approach to HIV, and analyzes the loss in rights and dignity that may accrue from a shift toward a population-level approach to prevention.

> To give the differend its due is to institute new addresses, new addressors, new significations, and new referents in order for the wrong to find an expression and for the plaintiff to cease being a victim . . . . What is at stake in a literature, in a philosophy, in a politics perhaps, is to bear witness to differends by finding idioms for them.
>
> —Lyotard, *The Differend* 13

In the months leading up to the 18th International AIDS Conference, held in Vienna in July 2010, through that year's International AIDS Day (1 December), politicians, researchers, and reporters amplified their use of rights language to describe solutions to the AIDS epidemic (International Centre for Science in Drug Policy). Indeed, the very name of the 18th Annual conference—Rights

Here, Right Now—suggested that a line had been drawn in the sand concerning the civil and legal plight of those subject to HIV/AIDS. Resonating with slogans and street protests from the early AIDS activist movement, reportage was laced with phrases that underscored a sense of urgency about conveying rights as a mechanism for combating a global disease. But what is the nature of the rights on offer, and to whom will these rights be given? We will see in the analysis that follows that there are in fact two ontologically incommensurable conceptualizations of the "rights" that are explicit or implicit in the current shift in AIDS policy, and these are specifically related to propositions about the role of HIV medications—"treatment"—in the global epidemic. I characterize these two relationships to rights as "witnessing illness" and "witnessing disease," and I measure the distance between these two ideas of rights by historicizing the rise of scientific and political consensus that undergird these witnessing positions as they are used to underwrite the two approaches to managing global HIV. The established approach voiced at the highest level with the World Health Organization (WHO), is exemplified in this essay by WHO's "3 million on HIV medications by the year 2005," program ("3 by 5"). This approach was developed in specific local contexts with differing histories and cultures of conceptualizing rights, but it generally weaves together two approaches to rights: (1) the Universal Declaration of Human Rights (UDHR) understanding and style of rights, which holds that fundamental conditions are necessary to life and (2) the post–World War II American legal concept of civil rights, which holds that minority groups able to demonstrate a pattern of discrimination will be accorded protections so that they may participate in the mode of living shared by the majority. WHO Director General Margaret Chan develops this understanding of rights and health in her WHO World AIDS Day statement:

> Health, HIV and human rights are inextricably linked. HIV responses need to ensure that human rights are protected and promoted. At the same time, the promotion and protection of human rights reduces HIV risk and vulnerability and makes HIV programmes more effective. Those populations most vulnerable and at risk of HIV are often the same populations prone to human rights violations. HIV policies and programmes in the health sector must promote human rights and empower individuals to exercise their rights . . . .
>
> People living with HIV should not only enjoy their right to health but also their right to access crucial social services such as education, employment, housing, social security and even asylum in some cases . . . . Working with people living with HIV is critical for an effective HIV response and Member States need to be mindful of the commitments made in the 2006 [United Nations] Political Declaration on HIV/AIDS to promote better legal and social environments for people to access HIV testing, prevention and treatment. (Chan)

Incommensurable with this hard won and nearly three-decade-old approach to health and human rights in the context of AIDS is the newly minted rubric of treatment-as-prevention. While this concept is by no means new to population health approaches, its implementation in the context of HIV is promoted as a "new paradigm," exemplified in this essay by the "Seek and Treat" program (S and T) in British Columbia where I live.[1] The press releases about the program and the single modeling paper published in a conventional academic journal, use language that superficially resonates with UDHR, but then employ the logic of population health to argue for the superiority of S and T over existing rights-conscious, risk assessment-based approach to prevention and access to care that has been the global standard for more than a decade. The architects of the scheme make no link to the decades of international debate about the range of rights explicitly embedded in the 3 by 5 implementation, debates in which AIDS-related organizations and persons living with AIDS played a major role. Instead, epidemiologic concepts quickly appear in place of more conventional rights talk: population substitutes for humanity, at-risk group for minority citizens.

It is as if the embodied participation—the witnessing illness—of persons with AIDS never happened.

Despite the massive local, national, and international media publicity about S and T, often accompanied by photos of scientist/clinicians with empathic faces and entreaties about the plight of the "hard to reach," the modeling paper—"Expanding access to HAART: a cost-effective approach for treating and preventing HIV"—give a rather different impression of the goals of the program:

> Objective: HIV continues to present a substantial global health burden. Given the high direct medical costs associated with the disease, prevention of new transmission is an important element in limiting economic burden . . . . In addition to providing therapeutic benefit, treatment with HAART has potential to prevent transmission of HIV. The objective in this study was to perform an economic

[1]The Canadian Centre for Excellence in HIV/AIDS, located in Vancouver, BC, is one of the several research groups that created the computer models used to argue for the economic and prevention value of the treatment-as-prevention approach. In order to test their model, the Centre for Excellence influenced the Provincial government to shift the existing constellation of HIV services into a program called "Seek and Treat for Optimal Prevention of HIV/AIDS." Several policy changes apparently related to S and T occurred as the program hit the ground: (1) deletion of the law that assured confidentiality for those with a contagious disease, (2) directions to doctors to offer HIV testing to any sexually active person, and without the pre-test and post-test counselling required for more than a decade under the BC Centres for Disease control policies, and (3) widespread use of a newly licensed "instant" test for HIV. The test, which in some sites is offered anonymously, has a high false positive rate (1–7% of positives are incorrect), requiring those who test positive to retest through conventional—and now no longer confidential—channels. It is not clear whether those who test negative receive any post-test counseling, a missed opportunity from the standpoint of education and prevention (BC Centre for Excellence in HIV/AIDS FORECAST; *About Seek and Treat*; Stop HIV/AIDS).

evaluation of the incremental net benefit associated with an intervention to expand treatment with HAART in British Columbia, Canada.

Results: Over 30 years, the HAART expansion scenario was associated with a net benefit of US$ 900 million . . .

Conclusion: Increasing the HAART treatment rate from 50 to 75% of clinically eligible individuals in British Columbia appears to be a cost-effective strategy based on this model. (Johnston, Levy and Lima)

The dehumanizing language, in which persons living with AIDS are potential transmission points associated with cost units, is not salvaged by the researchers' truncated view of rights as merely questions of vulnerability, consent, and voluntary participation. If citations in an article indicate what literatures researchers have examined, then the modeling team has ignored the volumes of social science research exploring how prevention works in practice, not to mention the wealth of humanistic representations (films, plays, novels, periodicals, and personal writings) that clearly and loudly articulate persons living with AIDS' views on questions of access and rights.[2] And of course, many scientists are skeptical: some argue that the models do not accurately reflect actual behavior, including the ability to maintain drug regimines, of persons to be enrolled in such programs (Wilson; Epstein; Adam; Wang, Ge, and Luo; J. Cohen; M. Cohen). Others question the feasibility of mass, voluntary testing programs, and/or inducements to keep positive persons on HIV medications for life (Jürgens, Cohen, and Tarantola; Hseih and De Arazoza). Yet others argue that the model is not falsifiable (the means of scientific proof) because of the extreme ontological difference between measuring behavioral and biomedical outcomes, or because the projected time of "success" is between 5 and 50 years into the future—in practical terms, implementing pilots programs based on the models essentially creates a new prevention and care regime; that is, it is a policy decision (Cohen, Mastro, and Cates Jr; Jaffe, Smith, and Hope; Rosengarten and Michael; Nguyen, Bajos, and Dubois-Arber).

[2] In an alternate version of the modeling article, authors ignore the many reasons persons avoid medical surveillance. Instead of assessing the impact of colonialism, homophobia, and drug policy—issues widely explored in the social science work on AIDS since the mid-1980s—researchers paint the dispossessed as irrational:

> . . . there are tremendous challenges associated with this initiative [Seek and Treat], given that a substantial number of individuals eligible for treatment will come from the pool of those marginalized and not engaged in care. The HAART expansion based on the 2008 IAS-USA guidelines will therefore require the development of a sustained and intensified strategy to identify HIV infected individuals and those at risk, helping them to stabilize their lives and facilitate their sustained engagement in appropriate health care and support, all of this within a voluntary and fully consented framework. These individuals are usually suffering from mental illnesses, addiction and poverty, thus complicating their access to proper health care, as it is the case of a large number of Aboriginal peoples and injection drug users. (Hogg, Lima, and Montaner 2010)

In order to get a hint of how we arrived as this space of incommensurability, in which parties disagree about the nature and degree of rights violations that might occur under treatment-as-prevention regimes, I identify the genesis of the concept of rights in AIDS-related community activism in the 1980s, acknowledging that the particular genealogy I offer is radically incomplete. I cannot overstate the importance of the many lawyers, human rights, and civil rights activists who were involved globally in the development of the early WHO response to AIDS. Well known local battles and negotiations in Nepal, Brazil, Uganda, Australia, Taiwan and Cuba, and no doubt other in places, resulted in a negotiated language of rights which incorporates local visions and concerns. As Eurocentric as is the human rights discourse in which such international collaborations do their work, when compared to the technocratic Western science whose statistical simulation of population is historically intertwined with a eugenicist impulse, the bricolage of interests assembled underneath the UN proclamations remain the most viable, or at least the most continuous, for creating the linkage that might begin to level the global health playing field (Said).

My investigation of the use of "rights" concepts will likely be orthogonal to the work undertaken in the legal world. My task here is to demonstrate how the scientists who promote the S and T bend rights language to imply that their research supports a larger moral consensus, even when it is clear that the implementation of their programs violate existing legal provisions designed to protect rights. Two conceptual substitutions enable me to avoid using some of the language and concepts of scholars who consider rights as legal or convention-based provisions to which one can point. First, I will mark the difference between overarching and often vague rights principles—for example, those in the UDHR—and the specific legislation and case law that establish or extend specific anti-discrimination provisions conceptualized as "enforceable" and "unenforceable rights."[3] I understand both enforceable and unenforceable rights to stand in contrast to a larger wrong that is (as yet) unhearable by those who activate systems of legitimation—in this case, those who say what is proper science. I draw on Jean-Francois Lyotard's distinction between damages—covered by the "genre" of enforceable rights claims—and wrongs, those violations that have no genre, or as he puts it: "This is what a wrong would be: a damage accompanied by the loss of the means to prove the damage" (Lyotard, *The Differend* 5).

These terminological shifts are in service of the larger distinction that might help us stay attuned to wrongs being committed in the *language of rights* when that language is detached from the longstanding concepts and consensuses that guided

[3]In Canada, you may not be evicted from your residence because you are a member of any number of "minority" groups; however, you have no underlying enforceable right to housing; that is, the government cannot be compelled to make good on its signature to decades of international proclamations that concern the right to housing.

the development and implementation of health-related laws, however problematic and limited those may be. There are two ontologically incommensurable forms of witnessing that underwrite the different forms of rights claims made in the current debates about HIV prevention. *Witnessing illness* requires the ongoing presence of the persons who are ill, as in the claims to dignity by the early persons with AIDS. *Witnessing disease* is the observation of the epidemic from the point of view of those who imagine themselves not subject to the disease, a disembodied meta-vision characteristic both of epidemiologists and research scientists who "see" the epidemic through statistical means, and also of the public officials who deploy that science as policy by speaking from the point of view of "the public."[4] I hope to show how witnessing disease transformed the actual once-speaking bodies of persons living with AIDS into "vulnerable groups" embedded in a larger population, where they experience loss of rights and an inability to articulate wrongs.

"We the Living": Witnessing Illness

Rights of People with AIDS

1. To live as full and satisfying sexual and emotional lives as anyone else.
2. To receive quality medical treatment and quality social service provision without discrimination of any form, including sexual orientation, gender, diagnosis, economic status or race.
3. To obtain full explanation of all medical procedures and risks, to choose or refuse their treatment modalities, to refuse to participate in research without jeopardizing their treatment and to make informed decisions about their lives.
4. To ensure privacy and confidentiality of medical records, to receive human respect and the right to choose who their significant others are.
5. To die—and to LIVE—in dignity. (People With AIDS Self-Empowerment Movement)

The initial wave of American AIDS activism was heavily indebted to the gay activism of the 1970s, in which two strands of homosexual activism took aim at

[4]According to Foucault, the notion of the "public" emerges in the eighteenth century as a dimension of the new concept of population, at once biological, as in the shift from humankind to human species, and political; public is "population seen under the aspect of its opinions, ways of doing things, forms of behavior, customs, fears, prejudices, and requirements" (75). The biological dimension of population—and the word—has been absorbed by demography and epidemiology, while law and politics absorbed the "public." Twentieth-century human rights activism has also privileged the latter, attempting to reincorporate the biological aspect of human being in reproductive and health rights. The incomplete re-suturing of these two aspects of population enables policymakers to argue that population health programs are good for all individuals within a population, so good, that the individual rights persons might wish claim are more limited, and therefore, lesser rights.

different targets.[5] The gay liberation movement's predominantly cultural critique argued that hetero-sexism was a form of colonialism that suppressed the libidinal and affective creativity of all persons. Gay liberationists were not indifferent to the idea that legal changes might be required, but, heavily influenced by Second Wave feminism, they sought instead to develop utopian relationships outside the family, the church, and the state which they argued were irredeemable institutions of sexual oppression. In contrast, gay rights activists endorsed the political vision of an ever-improving American democracy; enforceable rights and enumerated obligations of citizens were rightfully the property of openly homosexual persons, who, other than a detail of their desires, were just like everyone else. Both styles of activists responded quickly to the emergent health crisis in 1980, with no inkling that they (we) were witnessing a brightly burning moment of a medical *longue durée*; it was impossible to imagine the forms of coalitions across gender, cultural, political, and economic differences that would be required on the ground, nor was it yet clear that new forms of counter-expertise would be needed to engage, in particular, scientific systems of power. Of utmost importance to both styles of activism was bearing witness not only to illness but also to the wrongs that prevented compassionate governmental response, that exacerbated the plight of those who were first to fall ill, and that made safe sex organizing difficult.

Smack in the middle of what the media called the "gay plague," the young activists witnessed illness and death among their friends and lovers; they perceived the negative or ineffective social and governmental response to AIDS as a generalized attack on their fledgling community. In the face of right wing proclamations that AIDS was God's revenge for the "gay lifestyle," gay liberationists found it increasingly difficult to get political traction for their ideals of sexual freedom. But an early pamphlet, published at the same moment as the NAPWA declaration above, offered a disease-prevention strategy that would soon be called "safe sex."

> what began as sexual freedom has become a tyranny of sexually transmitted diseases.... Finding ways to have sex and avoid these epidemics might seem impossible, but we believe it's not. This pamphlet offers one means of reducing (and hopefully eliminating) risk which has yet to receive proper attention: limiting what sex acts you choose to perform to ones which

[5] This "initial period of AIDS activism" began in approximately 1981, with the recognition of a new, as-yet unnamed syndrome and stretched through 1984, when a virus was identified and linked as the prime, but not sufficient cause of the syndrome. As AIDS emerged in other regions of the world, the local histories of gender, sexuality, health, and development activism intertwined with the new question of AIDS. These important local, national, and regional histories shaped AIDS activism on the global scale, reverberating creative and hybrid responses. However, only the responses that most closely resembled the imaginings of "local activism" were publicized in publications and conferences, and eventually articulated by WHO as "best practices" to be taken up directly by national or local groups.

> interrupt disease transmission.... The key to this approach is modifying what you do—not how often you do it nor with how many different partners.... Our challenge is to figure out how we can have gay, life-affirming sex, satisfy our emotional needs, and stay alive! (Callen and Berkowitz)

This general philosophy became backbone of community-generated safe sex organizing (as opposed to later individualistic behavior change campaigns). But soon, witnessing illness in the form of attempting to sustain meaningful life was imperiled. At the margins of highly publicized legal violations against persons with AIDS who were thrown out of hospitals, sent home from their schools, or evicted from housing, the 1987 Helms Amendment (which denied federal health funding to any organization or group that "promoted promiscuity or homosexuality") generated a legal battle over what forms of educational message were permissible, a form of censorship which was added to international aid packages, and which still haunts safe sex work today. The vilification of gay sex placed whole communities under attack; gay men were fired or suspended from their jobs (especially in schools and hospitals) because their employers linked homosexuality with the dreaded AIDS. With few state or municipal protections for sexual minorities, and none on the federal level, advocates scrambling to gain a foothold against the discrimination circulating around AIDS, turned to the emerging body of disability law, ultimately codified in the 1990 federal Americans with Disabilities Act (ADA).

The turn to disability law was a critical legal milestone in codifying enforceable rights for persons living with AIDS, but only insofar as AIDS remained a stigmatized disease with a clear-cut link between a diagnosis and disability. Treatments that eventually enabled many to live with HIV as a chronic remitting disease complicated their ability to access disability benefits. As a result, additional legal activity was required to determine when disability law applied and when it did not. The social linkage between HIV-as-a-disability and homosexuality-as-a-disease enabled a new form of homophobia; because there were still few protections for lesbians and gay men as such, and because hate crime statutes were hard to enforce, the forms of social hatred and lack of freedom (wrongs as opposed to rights) analyzed by gay liberationists remained as a penumbra to the HIV-protections in the law.

As the new millennium dawned, the generalized idea of rights for persons with AIDS was largely accepted in democratic countries and by international health organizations, but the enforceability of these rights depended on disability or health-care related law. In some locales persons with AIDS were no longer burdened by the requirement to perpetually demand their rights in the streets; their right to care and freedom from housing, workplace, and some other forms of discrimination had become enforceable in the law. But almost no countries (post-Apartheid South Africa is a brilliant exception) made legal changes to explicitly address the questions of discrimination and stigmatization based in gender, sexual orientation, ethnicity, race, etc. in order to combat the social patterns that underlay HIV infection and poor prognosis. Paradoxically, in establishing enforceable rights in the discourse of damages, the indictment of broad structural wrongs that was originally laminated to rights claims came unglued. Once the law spoke on behalf of a specific claimant, the referent group who experienced ongoing wrongs floated free. Having made the speech of the wronged unnecessary in the case of *enforceable* rights, the wronged have gone missing; no reliable witness can be found to speak on their own behalf.[6] Now, scientists and politicians could invoke their plight without pointing to a specific government or person as the perpetrator of the wrongs, and they did so specifically in the rhetorical slide from juridical "humanity" to epidemiologic "population," severing analyses of structural harm from the testimony of victim witnesses and instead speaking on behalf of the health of the whole.

Witnessing Disease: Public Understandings of Science

In June and July of 1981, the U.S. Centers for Disease Control (CDC) released two sketchy accounts of otherwise healthy persons presenting with a rare and poorly understood pneumonia (pneumocystic pneumonia) or an aggressive version of a known, but usually slow-progressing cancer (Kaposi's sarcoma). Among the many thousands of curious, aberrant, and alarming cases of disease and injury investigated each year by the CDC, these cases were quickly grouped together because they were reported from a single region, among people who should not have gotten sick, and whom investigators believed or knew were homosexually active. Although the CDC was very cautious in noting this latter suspicion, the media immediately placed this possibility front and center in their reporting with headlines like "gay plague."

Although some researchers believed the syndrome resulted from the "fast lane lifestyle" of gay men (too many drugs, sexually transmitted diseases [STDs], and possibly even a reaction against other men's semen), oncologists almost

[6]Lyotard opens *Le Differend*:

> 1. You are informed that human beings endowed with language were placed in a situation such that none of them is now able to tell about it. Most of them disappeared then, and the survivors rarely speak about it. When they do speak about it, their testimony bears only upon a minute part of this situation. How can you know that the situation itself existed? That it is not the fruit of your informant's imagination? Either the situation did not exist as such. Or else it did exist, in which case your informant's testimony is false, either because he or she should have disappeared, or else because he or she should remain silent, or else because, if he or she does speak, he or she can bear witness only to the particular experience he had, it remaining to be established whether this experience was a component of the situation in question. (3)

immediately hypothesized a link to a newly defined class of proteins called retroviruses, already under study in animals with a similar pattern of health decline. Over the next three decades, scientists working from the retrovirus hypothesis would describe in great detail the characteristics and genetic composition of retroviruses and make important discoveries in endocrinology and oncology. This work, heavily indebted to the simultaneous work in genomics and the new field of proteomics, revolutionized scientific thinking about the cause, progression, and potential containment of disease.

Popular ideas about AIDS and disease in general did not change so quickly: the idea that a virus could attack the immune system was novel, while the idea that homosexuality, only removed from the list of psychiatric disorders in 1978, was "sick" was must easier to take in. How to explain to the public that what initially appeared to be a classic, if especially fatal, infectious disease, now proved to be a long term and complex decline in immune function related to a newly discovered class of virus? This long road might have begun by reinforcing the idea that viruses must no longer be thought of as inert hunks of matter, as baby boomers would have been taught in high school, but rather as building blocks whose reproduction trajectory entailed linking into and possibly fouling host RNA or DNA.

A decisive moment in the growing public misunderstanding of science occurred on 23 April 1984 when Secretary of Health and Human Services Margaret Heckler, a lawyer with little experience in health or human services whom Reagan had appointed for political reasons, announced that the U.S. had discovered the virus that caused AIDS; that a test for the "AIDS" would be forthcoming; and that a vaccine would soon follow, perhaps in only a year or two. Although scientists quickly raised doubts about her timeframe, since no one even understood how the retrovirus worked, much less how to stop it, they nevertheless filed patent applications not only for various forms of HIV tests but for also for both classic and novel forms of vaccine.[7] The blow to public curiosity was fatal: America's top health official, witnessing disease in the form of misunderstood science, promised a vaccine, so mainstream Americans might as well put the whole epidemic out of mind. The affected groups were viewed as largely separate from everyone else: even if it took a while to contain the epidemic among them, it was unlikely to "leap out" and affect "mainstream" society. But social prejudice was not the only factor in play: public misunderstanding of retrovirology left in place the idea that the promised vaccine would work like any other.

The second decisive moment in the widening gap between scientific and popular understanding occurred with the 1987 announcement of the first approved "AIDS drug," zidovudine or azidothymidine, commonly called AZT. The media's

[7]HIV antibody tests, and by the late 1990s, viral load tests, are unfathomably lucrative as the epidemic stretches out in space and time. If mass testing becomes the norm there will be a huge market, with many repeat customers: positive people will stop testing, but negatives keep coming back for more.

exuberant descriptions of the drug gave no hint of the problems in treating HIV. First, AZT was quite noxious and would quickly prove to be inadequate on its own. (AZT would, nevertheless, have a long life in combination therapies, especially after its patent expired in 2005 and it could be manufactured in generic form). Second, researchers still knew little about what happened between initial infection, the body's attempt to mount a response, and incremental collapse of the immune system: perhaps big doses early in this process ("hit early, hit hard" in the parlance of the day), could actually get rid of HIV. But there was not really a way to test this possibility, since the vast majority of people contracted HIV through sexual or drug use activities in which they engaged frequently: knowing with any precision when someone had been infected was nearly impossible.

But there were two researchable scenarios in which the exact moment and source of exposure was known: health care workers who had a needle stick accident with blood known to be HIV+ and the fetuses of HIV+ women. The first case was easy to transform into a quasi-experiment on the prophylactic use of AZT. The second was initially more difficult since women had been excluded from the AZT toxicity and efficacy clinical trials, and so it was unclear whether they (and their fetuses) could tolerate the "hit early, hit hard" dose. However, the assumption that pregnant women would or should wish to protect their fetus enabled mass testing programs to be piloted and eventually almost universally accepted (although not without considerable advocacy and monitoring by human rights activists), and this acceptance laid the groundwork for subsequent trials of the off-label use of AZT post-exposure prophylaxis (PEP).[8]

In the complicated melange of clinical ideals and practices spinning out after Heckler's claims, research on AZT as both a treatment for the infected, and as a means of post-exposure prophylaxis eroded the line between treatment and vaccination. This was not just a case of one drug being used in two different ways: the social meaning and legal status of vaccination is quite different from that of treatment. Vaccination policy debates recognize that vaccines will harm some individuals ("side effects") but this possibility is systematically minimized in order to achieve public compliance and thereby an adequate level of immunization across the population. Reduction in "new infections" is the measure of immunization success.[9] In the case of disease treatment, researchers study the superiority of

[8]Once a drug has been approved, it can—and often is—used informally to treat something that is not on its "label," hence the term "off label usage." For example, aspirin is given as "heart attack prevention." The ability to identify and then apply for patent extensions for secondary uses increases a company's market share. HIV Post-exposure prophalaxis (PEP) is currently used (in some places) off-label for women who had been raped, occasionally for gay men who report having a safe sex accident, and, by 2010, was being researched to give to people who are not infected, but were judged likely to become so (Grant and Lama).

[9]"Herd immunity" exists when enough individuals are vaccinated against a disease that the unvaccinated have lower odds of becoming infected simply because there is less chance of encountering an infected person. Public health officials aim for a vaccination rate that most effectively reduces population wide transmission: the exact dynamics of this process are the basis for developing vaccination campaign strategies.

one drug over another, judging the best to be the one that works for most individuals. These treatments may well have side-effects, but the decision about whether to tolerate them is left up to the patient: he can put up with a drug, or try to survive without it.

The early experimentation using treatments as quasi-vaccination were only one part of the overall failure of governments and media to make clear the revolution in disease conceptualization apparent in HIV science. The public (and, perhaps most importantly, policy makers) remained hazy about the mechanics of the HIV as an agent, the nature and effects of the drugs designed to block HIV replication (the "treatments" to which one has a right), and the plausibility of an HIV vaccine. Once the new combination therapies were refined in their applications in first-world contexts, it was easy to leap over all of the real complexities of HIV (rapid mutation of virus in some persons on drugs, the need to change drug combinations when first line drugs failed, and of course, the extent of the side effects to which those taking HIV drugs—as a treatment or as a prophalaxis would experience) and tout a new paradigm for HIV prevention, which required only that those who are infected discover this new fact about themselves and take a drug.

Witnessing Illness: Global Consensus, Local Implementation

If one read only the debates about treatment-as-prevention, with its ambition to "stop AIDS" everywhere, one might have the impression that no one has ever tried to craft a global response to AIDS. In 2003, following decades of small-scale efforts to get drugs to those who need them, and to negotiate policy consensus among constituent nations and the pharmaceutical industry, the UNAIDS and the WHO launched the "Treating 3 million by 2005," or 3 by 5 program, which had the

> global TARGET to provide three million people living with HIV/AIDS in low- and middle-income countries with life-prolonging antiretroviral treatment (ART) by the end of 2005. It was a step towards the GOAL of making universal access of HIV/AIDS prevention and treatment accessible for all who need them as a human right. (World Health Organization)

The program was developed with keen attention to the difficulties of implementation. Rampant discrimination against those who test positive in hostile environments and the level of "in country" infrastructure for HIV testing and monitoring of those on medications required thinking about human rights and finding means to level the global economic playing field. Prevention advocates were concerned about what would happen to local prevention campaigns, which had been difficult everywhere because of the social stigma associated with HIV's main transmission routes, but nevertheless appeared to be partly successful in leveling or reducing the number of new cases documented in gay communities by the mid-1990s, and elsewhere by the time 3 by 5 had a significant uptake. The 3 by 5 included parallel efforts to "scale up prevention," conceptualized as behavioral, normative, and legal change, alongside the "scaling up" of HIV treatment. For all the flaws in 3 by 5 (see Patton "Global"), the language written into its protocols and guidelines require sensitivity to cultural complexity and mandate participation of persons with AIDS and their communities in designing local programs. This "soul" of the 3 by 5 program is a direct outcome of the decades of brave persons with AIDS—and especially gay men and prostitutes—around the globe willingly making their faces and voices visible, and of ongoing diligence within WHO to promote a broad-based approach to grappling with the larger social and political forces that fuel or slow the HIV pandemic.

What has been the success of this program, with its expansion of treatment alongside initiatives to change behaviors, change social conditions, and improve medical care? According to the UNAIDS/WHO *09 AIDS Epidemic Update*, globally aggregated new infections are down 17% since 2001, with higher reductions in China and a leveling in Eastern Europe (where the epidemic began later). ARV coverage rose from 7% to 42% since the initiation of the 3 by 5 program in 2003. There is no question that progress has been slow; nevertheless, 3 by 5 awkwardly manages to balance the promotion and activation of enforceable rights with achieving health for persons. In the 3 by 5 framework, prevention is a community-level activity undertaken by actual, located persons who possess valuable insights and a deep investment in the lifeways of their community; treatment is critical to preserving health, but it is a technical intervention at the level of the cell.

If 3 by 5 was built by something resembling, if not a democratic process, than an intersectoral consensus, and if it is proving successful on the ground, then why did some scientists and policymakers begin to promote treatment as prevention, since that approach requires modification of provisions related to confidentiality in testing and treatment, and will certainly require intensified surveillance of potentially non-compliant HIV+ persons, a scrutiny that the "hard-to-reach" are hardly likely to welcome? What justifies a retreat from hearing the embodied witnessing of persons living with HIV who still speak loudly about their desires for control over their own programs, for justice, for rights?

Although superficially cloaked in rights-resonant language, the treatment-as-prevention approach quickly slides from "vulnerable populations" to "at-risk populations" to actuarial claims about the number of "infections" the program might avert and at what dollar investment and savings, with little further consideration of the realities of living with HIV on the ground. This disembodied *witnessing disease* occurs in the use of epidemiological language—hard to reach (by whom?) and at-risk people (of HIV only?)—and this use of science cannot readily be contested in the language of *witnessing illness*. It becomes impossible to hear the pleas of those who remain locked out of the "crucial social services such as education, employment, housing, social security and even asylum" (Chan), those "hard to reach" a la Seek and Treat, who are the real and identifiable persons the 3 by 5 program seeks to empower. Attempting to speak within science's genre of falsification, those who witness illness seem partial and subjective; what they say is not considered evidence and may not even audible as testimony at all. Witnessing disease sees prevention on the level of population, and populations do not speak except in the language of "the public," already constituted in AIDS discourse as the "to be protected" in relationship to the "bodies to be protected against." Because witnessing disease claims its superiority on the basis of population-level viral reduction and cost, treatment-as-prevention programs cannot "see" the individual. When the individual is subsumed into the population in which aggregate viral load is to be reduced by the suppression of virus through drugs, we should be very clear about whose bodies will come under scrutiny, both as potentially HIV positive, and if positive, as the vessels of requisite treatment-for-life.

Witnessing Wrongs

> Reflection requires that you watch out for occurrences, that you don't already know what's happening. It leaves open the question: Is it happening?
>
> (Lyotard, *The Differend* 5)

Almost thirty years ago the suffering bodies of persons living with AIDS demanded that structures of power recognize them as full persons: they witnessed an ongoing wrong to which they were subject. Because it was—and remains—necessary to work within the laws of specific nations, the wrong—literally fatal social stigma and indignity—endures despite the responses from many governments in the form of rights legislation and confidentiality protections (developed under great pressure from the wronged).

The truncation of the demanded right to dignity into a conveyed right to treatment read through the lens of uncontested and falsely promised scientific solutions laid the moral groundwork for the apparent appeal of treatment-as-prevention programs, as if they have the same broad ambitions as the universal access programs. Treatment-as-prevention programs require testing and mandatory treatment on a scale seen only in dictatorships. If carefully constructed press campaigns convince vast numbers of people to "voluntarily" submit to testing and, if found positive, undergo lifelong treatment, this "success" will be at the cost of a very different global consensus about how to manage health across the deep trenches of wealth and poverty, an effort that requires coordinated programs crafted between philanthropists, foreign aid, governments, and, yes, pharmaceutical companies to improve the health infrastructure of poor countries in order to deliver even simplified versions of HIV medications. The treatment-as-prevention approach overrides classic enforceable rights of individuals (confidentiality, right to treatment decision making, anti-discrimination), and ignores the international consensus that weak countries have a collective right to self-determination, two forms of rights underpinning the myriad programs that seek to equalize development and infrastructure resources across the globe.

In the uncanny moment of the shock and awe of a statistical modeling that cloaks itself in the ethos of rights, how can we remain attentive to the possibility of the wrongs that will be incurred upon individuals who will be the "targets" of a program? Lyotard proposes that we remain attentive to the possible presence of a differend, to cases of incommensurability in how values can be proposed. His rhetorical model of ethics implicitly encourages us to remember that rights must be conveyed by someone, to someone, in some context. Even if it is popular for everyone to invoke "rights," rights only take on meaning relationally, most of all when they have force for those who claim them (whether that is only in law, or more broadly, in a call to be attentive to effects of policy). We should attend closely to the difference between witnessing illness, which remains focused on the individual's course of disease, her daily triumphs and set backs, her transition from an initial acute illness to illness chronicity, to the break into the reality of the end-stage, and witnessing disease, which focuses on decreasing the disease phenomenon as a whole, and scaling back and forth from case (as opposed to individual) to population (as distinct from humanity) with the assumption that an overall improvement in health "scales down" equally to all members of society. As I have tried to show here, there is not only an epistemological gap in how the two forms of witnessing "know" about disease, there is also an ontological gap that affects the ability to make claims: a population cannot meaningfully be said to "suffer," and yet contemporary calls to be better global citizens are founded directly on the articulation of individual human suffering. This disconnect should alert us to the presence of "something wrong" even if we lack the power to speak back to science. We should never allow costing arguments to cloak themselves in the language of human rights. Implementation of large programs requires money, but more than money, health programs on the global scale require political consensus. We should beware of claims by powerful institutions to speak on behalf of the vulnerable: entering the affected into models as "vulnerable groups" is not the same as seeking to hear the speech of the wronged. We should never allow wrongs to be enumerated in financial terms: justice is justice, regardless of the price tag. When we find ourselves numbered among the beneficiaries of a population-level health intervention, we must look closely at the dynamics of the disease: who among us will carry the largest burden for ensuring the safety of an "all" from which the burdened will, in effect, be excluded?

Is it happening?

References

Adam, Barry D. "Epistemic Fault Lines in Biomedical and Social Approaches to HIV Prevention." 2011. Unpublished manuscript.

BC Centre for Excellence in HIV/AIDS. *FORECAST.* Vancouver, 10 May 2010. Web. 18 December 2010. <http://www.cfenet.ubc.ca/news/forecast/may-2010>.

BC Centre for Excellence in HIV/AIDS. *About Seek and Treat.* nd. Web. 18 December 2010 <http://www.cfenet.ubc.ca/our-work/initiatives/seek-and-treat>.

Benjamin, Walter. n.d.

Callen, Michael, and Richard Berkowitz. *How to Have Sex in an Epidemic: One Approach.* New York: News From the Front Publications, 1983. Print.

Chan, Margaret. "Human rights—A Central Concern for the Global HIV Response." *World Health Organization.* 30 November 2010. Web. 10 December 2010. <http://www.who.int/mediacentre/news/statements/2010/AIDS_Day_20101130/en/index.html>.

Cohen, J. "The Ins and Outs of HIV." *Science* 327 (2010): 1196–1197. Print.

Cohen, Myron S. "HIV Treatment as Prevention: In the Real World the Details Matter." *Journal of Acquired Immune Deficiency Syndrome* 56.3 (2011): e101. Print.

Cohen, Myron S, Timothy D Mastro, and Willard, Jr. Cates. "Universal Voluntary HIV Testing and Immediate Antiretorviral Therapy." *The Lancet* 373 (2009): 1077. Print.

Foucault, M. *Security, Territory, Population (Lectures at the College Du France).* Eds. M. Senellart Trans and G. Burchell. New York: Palgrave Macmillan, 2007. Print.

Grant, Robert, and Javier R. Lama. "Preexposure Chemoprophylaxis for HIV." *New England Journal of Medicine.* 1 December 2010. Web. 10 December 2010 <www.NEJM.org>.

Hogg, Robert S., Viviane D. Lima, and Julio S. G. Montaner. "Expanding HAART Treatment to All Currently Eligible Individuals under the 2008 IAS-USA Guidelines in British Columbia, Canada." *PLOS One* 5.6 (2010): 1–7. Print.

Hseih, Ying-Hen, and Hector De Arazoza. "Universal Voluntary HIV Testing and Immediate Antiretroviral Therapy." *The Lancet* 373 (2009): 1079–1080. Print.

International Centre for Science in Drug Policy. *The Vienna Decleration.* n.d. Web. <http://www.viennadeclaration.com/the-declaration/>.

Jaffe, Harold, Adrian Smith, and Tony Hope. "Universal Voluntary HIV Testing and Immediate Antiretroviral Therapy." *The Lancet* 373 (2009): 1080. Print.

Johnston, Karissa M., Adrian R. Levy, Viviane D. Lima, Robert S. Hogg, Mark W. Tyndall, Paul Gustafson, Andrew Briggs, and Julio S. Montaner. "Expanding Access to HAART: A Cost-Effective Approach for Treating and Preventing HIV." *AIDS* 24 (2010): 1–8. Print.

Jürgens, Ralf, Jonathan Cohen, Daniel Tarantola, Mark Heywood, and Robert Carr. "Universal Voluntary HIV Testing and Immediate Antiretroviral Therapy." *The Lancet* 373 (2009): 1079. Print.

Lyotard, Jean François. *The Differend: Phrases in Dispute.* Trans. Georges Abbeele. Minneapolis: University of Minnesota Press, 1983/1988. Print.

Nguyen, Vinh-Kim, Nathalie Bajos, Françoise Dubois-Arber, Jeffrey O'Malley, and Catherine M. Pirkle. "Remedicalizing an Epidemic: From HIV Treatment as Prevention to HIV Treatment Is Prevention." *AIDS* 25 (2011): 291–293. Print.

Patton, Cindy. "Global Clinic? Scaling Up for HIV Treatment." *HIV/AIDS: Global Frontiers in Prevention/Intervention.* Ed. Cynthia Pope & Renee White. London, UK: Taylor and Francis, 2009. Print.

———. *Globalizing AIDS.* Minneapolis, MN: University of Minnesota Press, 2002. Print.

———. "Endemic Reporting: Calibrating the 'News' and 'Normal Disease'." *Global Media, Culture, and Identity.* Eds. Rohit Chopra and Radhika Gajjala. London: Routledge, 2011. 19–32. Print.

People With AIDS Self-Empowerment Movement. *The Denver Principles.* Denver, CO, 1983. Print.

Rosengarten, Marsha, and Mike Michael. "Rethinking the Bioethical Enactment of Medically Drugged Bodies: Paradoxes of Using Anti-HIV Drug Therapy as a Technology for Prevention." *Science as Culture* 18.2 (2009): 183–199. Print.

Said, Edward. *Culture and Imperialism.* New York: Knopf, 1993. Print.

Stop HIV/AIDS. *Project Updates: What Improvements have been made through the Stop HIV/AIDS Initiative?* Vancouver, BC: BC Centre for Excellence in HIV/AIDS, 2010. Print.

UNAIDS; WHO. *09 Aids Epidemic Update.* Geneva: Joint United Nations Programme on HIV/AIDS (UNAIDS), November 2009. Web. 18 December 2010. <http://www.unaids.org/en/dataanalysis/epidemiology/2009aidsepidemicupdate/>.

Wang, Lu, Zeng Ge, Jing Luo, Duo Shan, Xing Gao, Guo-Wei Ding, Jian-Ping Zhou, Wen-Sheng He, and Ning Wang. "HIV Transmission Risk Among Serodiscordant Couples: A Retrospective Study of Former Plasma Donors in Henan, China." *Journal of Acquired Immune Deficiency Syndrome* 55.2 (2010): 232–238. Print.

Wilson, David P. "Universal Voluntary HIV Testing and Immediate Antiretorviral Therapy." *The Lancet* 373 (2009): 1077–1078. Print.

World Health Organization. *World Health Organization 3 by 5 Initiative.* n.d. Web. 10 December 2010. <http://www.who.int/3by5/en/>.

A Question of Confession's Discovery

Erik Doxtader

What can be said in the aftermath? Faced with legacies of conflict and the gross violation of human rights, the contemporary discourse of transitional justice has defended the work of confession as a way for deeply divided societies to "come to terms" with the past and move forward. Underwritten by a complex promise of recognition, this call for confessional truth-telling has proven controversial, not least at it risks undermining the testimony of victims and granting undue status to perpetrators. Giving voice to events that may prove unspeakable and performing a subjectivity that may defy accountability, the figure of confession imagined by transitional justice is perhaps best envisioned as a rhetorical question, a difficult inquiry into the response-ability of language in the wake of violence.

In the aftermath, the difficult work of public testimony may include a question that verges on a demand, a request by those bearing witness that appears in the name of justice—*Who will tell me*? Heard at a moment and in a scene predicated on the need to listen, this query is compelling even as it rarely compels a satisfying reply. Beyond an inquiry for information and an explanation of cause—*What happened? At whose hands? On what order*?—this question may go further, perhaps inadvertently, and ask not simply for an account but an expression of accountability that amounts to a sign of recognition—*Why? By what right? On what grounds*? With this turn, testimony's query exposes a lacuna about which it is difficult to speak, the possibility that the survivor—as a survivor—can never fully bear witness.[1] Here, at this threshold, the question posed by the testifying subject—an "I" formed in the very struggle to give testimony—risks displacing the witness's own voice as it calls on an other to not only explain but assume the unspeakable violence that has been done to "me." *Who will tell me? Who will tell me—of me*? The slippage between these questions may amount to nothing less than a wound. If asking after the facts gives way to a query that prefigures a

[1]For important approaches to the question of testimony's impossibility, see Felman and Laub; Ross; Mandel; Agamben; Bernstein ("Bare Life").

relation, those that have suffered may be called to make an unjustifiable sacrifice (once again) to those that have done them harm, to those that have shown little concern for the difference between the interrogative gesture and the interrogation's violence—*I will not give standing let alone listen to the words of those who fashioned and then lived (all too well) with the lies that sustained barbarism.* As testimony pronounces the question of accountability, it confronts the potential for (ir)responsibility, an inquiry whose presupposition may warrant opposition to its expression.

In the name of human rights: testimony and confession. Victims of abuse, subjugation, and atrocity must be heard; perpetrators must come forward and disclose their "acts and omissions." If these are not new imperatives, at least when considered from within the confines of human rights discourse, the question of their (non)relation—we will need to insist on this ambivalence for (a) time—has been rendered urgent by the advent of transitional justice and its institutionalization in the contemporary human rights regime. An amalgam of academic inquiry, policy-making, and political (in)action, the discourse of transitional justice is addressed largely to the problem of how deeply divided and conflict-wracked societies can best make their way from past to future, from systemic violence to rule of law, from bitter fragmentation to democratic unity. In both theory and practice, this discourse is thus concerned with the ways that balkanized nations and shattered communities can "come to terms," a goal that has led transitional justice to reach beyond the aims of the tribunals that helped define the form and content of human rights doctrine in the mid-twentieth century. While the "New York consensus" that has endeavored in the last years to codify (and then enforce) the means and ends of transitional justice continues to stress the imperative of prosecuting those responsible for the gross violation of human rights, the end of the Cold War and the open wounds of colonialism demonstrated the need for a broader (and deeper) approach, a range of initiatives dedicated to gathering "as full a picture as possible" of the roots, motives, experiences and costs of conflict.[2] In these terms, transitional justice hopes for a full accounting and tangible accountability, a way of understanding and redressing the damage done that requires both listening to the experiences of victims and hearing the perspectives of perpetrators; only with contributions from all "sides" (a notion whose perceived leveling effect has provoked outrage) is it possible to explain the violence, reconstitute juridical-political order, deter revisionism, foreclose impunity, restore the dignity of victims and survivors, establish a referent for reparation, and build the foundations of human rights culture.

[2]The phrase "as full a picture as possible" plays a central role in the mandate of South Africa's Truth and Reconciliation Commission. The transitional justice literature is now vast, as is the network of organizations working under its banner. For insight into its motivations and methods, see Teitel ("Genealogy") and Elster.

As transitional justice would have it, even as the discourse of transitional justice is not particularly keen to admit it, the announced hope of "coming to terms" hinges on the arrival of words, an expansive and unpredictable process of telling and hearing from which no one is *de facto* excluded and that sets the testimony of victims and statements by perpetrators into proximity, a (non)relation that today appears most clearly within the confines of the contemporary truth commission.[3] Increasingly held out as a necessary component of transition, the work of these "quasi-juridical" bodies has been defined by a variety of mandates, many of which authorize the creation of public spaces for testimony and establish more or less formal incentives for individuals to come forward in the name of disclosing the terms, motivation, and extent of their crimes.[4] While the work of attending to the needs of victims and survivors has been applauded—at least in principle—the attending effort to promote confession and bring its gesture outside the courtroom has provoked difficult questions: In the wake of conflict, civil war, and atrocity, what do we want to hear from those that have committed, supported and benefited from the violation of human rights? What do we need to hear? What can we hear?

If the aftermath of historical violence demands a full picture, the hope for truth, transparency, and accountability becomes complicated when it is seen as a way of granting status to the presence and voice of the perpetrator, a position that may be neither justified nor just insofar as it overshadows the experiences of victims and survivors, blurs the difference between guilt and trauma, weakens the drive for prosecutions, and dilutes collective moral outrage. Articulated in response to an offer to bring a particular film into "conversation" with his own well-known work, Claude Lanzmann's adamant lack of interest in the experiences of Nazi officials illustrates the concern, a deep ethical-political worry that such accounts may presume to bridge the gap of understanding and thus degrade the significance of the Shoah by attempting to render it comprehensible.[5] While this view has been challenged on grounds that do not necessarily participate in the politics of denial, it is reflected in the way that academic literature tends to police the distance between inquiry into testimony and studies of perpetrator discourse.[6] Bolstering calls for the international community to embrace a "right to truth," the position also resonates with expressed worries as to whether truth commissions proceed from an ambiguous secular and religious authority (not least as they may advocate for various forms of reconciliation) whose interest in confession underwrites

[3]Hayner offers a useful introduction to the history of the modern truth commission. For a critical reflection on the issues at stake in these bodies, see Sanders.

[4]Beyond what I can address here, the incentives for such disclosures are tied to a bitter debate over the value of amnesty. See Rotberg and Thompson and, for a less legalistic view, see Villa-Vicencio.

[5]Also see Blanchot; Bernard-Donals and Glejzer; Friedlander; Mandel 55–69.

[6]For two studies that speak to the obstacles involved in approaching perpetrator discourse, see Foster et al. and Payne.

"perpetrator-friendly" forums that trade impunity for (pre)scripted accounts of imprescriptable crimes and that create incentives to declare that everyone is guilty.[7]

The confession is a fault line, a source of division within already divided societies (and the international human rights community) and a site of struggle within the discourse of transitional justice. Even under the "best" of circumstances, it is difficult to trust the confession's expression. As what was declared true (then) is retracted and deemed truly false (now), the confession seems to undermine its own veracity even as its self-betraying words appear to instantiate guilt. In this way, the confession is never far from the question of its hypocrisy, a question that asks after the operativity and integrity of the confession's performance and the integrity of its performativity. What is (to be) done with(in) the confession's speech action? What grounds (justify faith in) the power of the confession's word? To these inquiries, the discourse of transitional justice replies that the confessional gesture promises the potential for recognition, a disclosure and self-effacing bond of unifying words. Beginning with a brief reflection on how the confession's performance may obscure its performative dynamics, my aim in the following few pages is to unpack this promise and complicate its stakes: when it is grasped as a movement between an (un)speakable re-cognition of its object and the recognition of its (non)accountable subject, the confession exposes a question of (its) (ir)response-ability that is partly an inquiry into its hypocrisy and which may be less the basis for moral condemnation than the (re)turn and (re)turning of discovery, a question of language's ethical (im)potential in the face of its violence.

For a very long time, the power of confession's truth(fulness) has been pegged to its performative quality. As Augustine suggested, the confession relies not only on what is said but the manner in which it is spoken, a way of speaking that reveals the damage done and which brings those suffering the weight of sin back into relation with the (true) word.[8] In our own time, as he reflected on Rousseau, Paul de Man questioned whether *The Confessions* is in fact a "confessional text," and then held that, "To confess is to overcome guilt and shame in the name of truth: it is an epistemological use of language in which the ethical values of good and evil are superseded by values of truth and falsehood" (de Man 279). Looking closely at this claim, Derrida observes that the constative quality of confession, its concern for "stating things as they are" (de Man 279), cannot be easily distinguished from its illocutionary force; as de Man's own terms suggest, the confession's truth-telling appears to *supercede, overcome, restore*, and *redeem* the cognitive work

[7]An element of the recently ratified *Convention for the Protection of All Persons from Enforced Disappearances*, the right to truth is generally viewed as a non-derogable assurance that victims will receive "a disclosure of the whole and complete truth" about past human rights violations (Report 16).

[8]For useful commentaries see Smith; Taylor; Tell ("Beyond").

of "making known."[9] On this view, one that Derrida seeks to complicate, the confession becomes confessional only as its rhetorical performance of truth-telling unfolds with(in) an attending performative rhetoric that "produce[s] the event of which it speaks," constitutes a (guilty) mode of being, and alters the standing and relation of (non)speaking subjects.[10] More precisely, the traditional ethical-political promise of the confessional gesture is thought to take shape through words that stage a non-ironic (although potentially tragic) self-exposure, a giving (up) of truth through an expression whose declarative force is conditioned by a "passivity and dependence" that gives (away) the particularity of the self to an other.[11] Called to undertake a self-betraying speech act, the confessing subject relies on a grammar of self-certainty to announce the terms of its offense, a transgression whose appearance strips the grammar of its justification and thus (dis)places the confessor into a struggle for recognition.

Transitional justice has high hopes for this struggle. As it breaks the hard heart through the "'throwing away' of the self in relation to the other, that presages universality through dissimilarity" (Bernstein, "Confession," 48), the confession's performance offers the precise move to which transitional justice aspires, a turn from violent division to an abiding unity in difference that recalls one of confession's basic meanings in antiquity, the *homologia* that marks a "coming to correspond" with(in) words and a deep agreement borne of a speaking together in one language.[12] On Derrida's reading, however, this bond of self-effacing words may unravel its own pronounced promise. As he hears it, the confession both fires a machine and heralds an event, a co-production wherein the disclosure of "facts" that enlightens historical understanding risks committing to an identitarian and (re)iterable expression that conditions justice on a founding perjury *and* whereby the spontaneity needed to enact self-abasement for an other may be binding only as the relinquishment of self-certain words is indemnified by the very (rule of) law that the confession claims to challenge ("Typewriter," 125, 152). If so, Derrida concludes, "For there to be a confessional declaration or avowal, it is necessary, indissociably, that I recognize that I am guilty in a mode of recognition that is not of the order of cognition" ("Typewriter," 109). In other words, the confession's performance must—without compulsion and in one breath—set (its) recognition beside itself. If it is to amount to less than an "automatic repetition"

---

[9]See Derrida ("Typewriter" 108–111, 129). For a sense of the debate over how the constative presupposes the performative and, more directly, the question of whether confession's performance includes or exceeds the work of cognitive-logical demonstration, compare Derrida ("Typewriter") and Bernstein ("Confession"). On the question of how to distinguish between the truth and veracity of political interaction, including confession, see Arendt ("Truth") and Derrida ("History").

[10]See De Man (300) and Derrida ("University" 234); Foucault (*Hermeneutics* 327).

[11]Compare Bernstein ("Confession" 54) and Butler (Giving 35–37).

[12]For accounts of transitional justice that reflect on the performative quality of confession, see Moon; Teitel (*Transitional*); Payne; Cole.

and more than a self-retracting retraction, its power turns on the creation and (non)relation of an epistemic re-cognition and an ethical recognition, a disclosure of an unspeakable truth and a gesture of accountability that defies account.

What does this mean? And what are its concrete implications for the role of confession in the discourse of transitional justice, a discourse that has perhaps deployed an "imperative" for action to flatten and homogenize the idea of performance in the name of stabilizing the confession's inconsistent and internally divided rhetorical operations? In fashioning a reply, it is helpful to reflect first on the confession's beginning, a moment in which an interest in truth that "makes good" calls for(th) words about a (yet) unspoken and perhaps unspeakable violence, an infliction of suffering that degrades if not dehumanizes both its victim and its perpetrator, albeit in different ways—a controversial point to which I will return shortly. Here, whether it aims to disclose infraction or atrocity, the confession's voluntarism is inaugurated and conditioned by a register that delineates an offense and that does so in a manner which provokes the question of self-conscious expression, the ways in which the subject's infliction of injury calls for a disclosure that sets its standing into question (Butler *Giving* 10). Most often, this work of disclosure is given to law, a system of morality and justice that circumscribes action within a logic of transgression, culpability, guilt, retribution, and perhaps restoration. As Judith Butler has made clear, however, the law—whether sacred or secular—is not the only "interlocutory scene in which one is asked what one has done, or a situation in which one tries to make plain, to one who is waiting to know, what one has done, and for what reason" (13–14). Beyond the dock (and the booth), Butler suggests (11), the confession arrives with a question before which we wait: "Was it you?"

An inquiry arrives and asks after my role in "it." What can(not) be said in reply? Setting aside, for a moment, the status of the "I" that may or not "offer" a response, the question opens and delineates—with greater or lesser specificity—a historical grammar and vocabulary. It may do so partly through an archive, a (re)collection of forms that underwrite both what must be said in reply to the question of confession and how it is best said.[13] As Butler has suggested by way of Foucault, the question pre-figures its reply, not least as it calls for(th) the narration of a "causal relation to the suffering of others" or an articulation of motivation, the underlying or "emergent" conditions of action (12, 37). If so, the question with which the confession begins asks after (and provides) that which I cannot explain at the same time that it offers a way to compose a reply whose coherence may well be suspect (63). In her terms, the question defies a satisfying (true) answer: "To hold a person accountable for his or her life in narrative form

[13]In other words, the question relies on and evokes what Foucault called a "history of 'verdictions,' understood as the forms according to which discourses capable of being declared true or false are articulated concerning a domain of things" (*Aesthetics* 460). Also see Foucault ("Truth").

may even be to require a falsification of that life in order to satisfy the criterion of a certain kind of ethics, one that tends to break with relationality."[14]

All of this is difficult to hear, not least as it may also complicate the testimonial gesture in a very discomforting way. As it asks for a disclosure of my action, the question of confession is a request for a re-cognition, an epistemic provision or a representation of acts, offenses, and omissions that may remain unspeakable or that can be spoken only in a manner that renders (its) truth suspect. Thus, a disclosure limited to the facts as the perpetrator "knows" them may simply beg the question at hand or, it may proceed from within the very discourse that underwrote the violence under consideration. To confess on a register "beyond" this threshold, the confession's renouncement of self-certainty enjoins the confessor to proceed in unknown terms even as, at the same time, the expressed terms of the confession risk yet another wound: that is, the injunction that the unspeakable must remain as such, and that the event must not be corrupted with accounts that are necessarily inadequate but potentially normalizing, may obscure the risk that the words of perpetrators will overwrite the testimony of victims or replicate the logic used by the architects of the past regime to rationalize their evil (Haidu 294). At every point then, a double-bind, an undecidable question. The language provided by the question of confession's beginning cannot be trusted even as it may help diagnose the way in which violence distorts political-ethical (self) expression, a distortion that the confession may perpetuate, not least as it is limited to a re-cognition in which the recollection of particular actions and motives distracts from the incomprehensible magnitude of the general event or advances the deeply problematic suggestion that everyone is somehow a victim.[15]

When called by the question "Was it you?," do we say what happened or do we confront the happening as the very limit of what can be said? Whether deployed by truth commissions or used to warrant an international right to truth, the demand for a full disclosure rests on a power to name, a capacity to declare what has been done, to define the origins, intentions, and causes of violence, to set a precedent that can pre-empt the question of what can(not) be said and which may legitimize the continuity of positive law with blood on its hands. Yet, the decision to decline

[14]Butler (*Giving an Account* 63). The claim is made clearer with Butler's contention: "But, if I can address you, I must first have been addressed, brought into the structure of address as a possibility of language before I was able to find my own way to make use of it. This follows, not only from the fact that language first belongs to the other and I acquire it through a complicated form of mimesis, but also because the very possibility of linguistic agency is derived from the situation in which one finds oneself addressed by a language one never chose" (53). The question that follows is how this dynamic may also bear on the expression of the question that begins confession's work. In the closing moments of the essay, I return to this dilemma, not least by suggesting that the question that convenes testimony may need to remain open, a question as such.

[15]While she is addressing the "empty talk" of a defendant, Hannah Arendt's chronicle and critique of the *Eichmann* trial is wholly relevant here, not least for the way it plots how self-defined functionaries charged to carry out legal violence are bereft of meaningful words at the same time that "officialese" vocabularies occlude a grasp of their own violence (Eichmann 48).

this disclosure or claim that one does not know may amount to little more than a tactic that aims for impunity, the well-honed and cynical gambit of "confessing" to the "fact" that one simply "cannot recall" (Butler, *Giving* 116–117). The line between this approach and the confession's ethical potential is a fine one. Indeed, there may be no certain reply to the confession's opening question, only the tension between a plausibly deniable evasion of the word that repeats the offense to which it speaks and the handing over of language in the name of relinquishing the capacity to make a claim on an other.

For transitional justice, the question that announces the occasion of confession yields signs that point in different directions, a divergence that seems to defy coherent account: what is said cannot be spoken; speaking says too much and too little; what is reserved as unsayable condones an unspeakable wrong. If this ambiguity gives pause, it also underscores how the re-cognition of the confession's (un)speakable disclosure calls for(th) if not demands the recognition of an accountable subject. Recalling Derrida's claim that it "produces the event of which it speaks," the confession's object may hinge on the (re)making of the self, a "return to oneself, to be oneself, to be what one is, as an indivisible whole . . . ." ("Typewriter" 97). Or, as Butler describes the making of the sinner, "a certain performative production of the subject within established public conventions is required of the confessing subject and constitutes the aim of confession itself" (113). In short, the confession appears to turn the self around and against itself. Is this exercise a will to knowledge, an instrumentalizing self-accusation, or an ethical mode of (inter)action? Does it amount to an undue subjection or a potentially productive subjectivation? In the name of securing accountability for that which may resist disclosure, might it be both? And, if so, what does this work say about the confession's power of recognition?

Behind the portable and contested categories of perpetrator, collaborator, and beneficiary, the confession entails self-production. In his best known and likely most influential formulation, Foucault took this to mean that, within the confession, "the speaking subject is also the subject of the statement" (*History* 61). But, which statement? As Foucault continues, "the confession is also a ritual that unfolds within a power relationship, for one does not confess without the presence (or virtual presence) of a partner who is not simply the interlocutor but the authority who requires the confession, prescribes and appreciates it, and intervenes in order to judge, punish, forgive, console, and reconcile" (61). On this view, one that Foucault finds at the heart of Christianity, the confessor's performance is front-loaded; it is imbued and directed by an "agency of domination" that defines what it means to be(come) a confessing subject and figures the speech action of confession as an exposure of the self's limit, a "representation of death" that aims to discover, extract, and support truth through what Foucault calls the endless "verbalization" of sin (*Politics* 210, 223).[16] Having succumbed to sin's forgetting,

[16]Also see Butler, *Giving* 121–123.

the confessing subject is called to undertake a sacrifice of the self, an abandonment of words in the name of remembering and professing an allegiance to the Word. As the self gives itself away in the name of becoming a subject defined by the mining and display of an inner truth that is and is not its own, the confession's potential for accountability is reduced to a juridical and then a biopolitical operation (Foucault "Truth" 15, 44, 58). And yet, Foucault's later work weaves his view of the confession's "individualization by power" with threads that, if pulled just a bit, show the confession less as an involuntary renunciation than a relational "art" of testing. Cast as a hermeneutics of the self invested towards care and a concern for the emergence of ethical life, the task of such confession is to "become a subject of truth," a subject that is defined less by a constitutive force that discloses a "secret reality inside the individual" than a discovery that serves to "turn the individual into a place where truth can appear . . ."[17] Without conflating constitution and discovery, particularly as the autonomy promised by *parrhēsia* begins within an explicitly pedagogical (master–student) relationship that does not demand an acknowledgement of guilt so much as "open-heartedness," the *parrhesiastes* of antiquity suggests that the confessional form can unfold as a kind of "self-publishing." Through confession, words yield an appearance of the self before others, a manifestation and perhaps even a demonstration of who the self *is* that dispossesses the self of its certainty insofar as its expression performs its dependence on others (Butler *Giving* 112–113). Such a confession, the *logos* of confession, marks the discovery of *ethos*, a risking of self for the self, a self-relinquishment that may count not so much as domination as a productive mode of (de)humanization, a turn in which the loss of language provokes the question of how to (re)compose its ethical power.[18]

If its beginning holds the question of (its) (un)speak-ability, the confession struggles equally with the (non)account-ability of (its) self-betrayal, a manifestation of guilt that moves beyond the re-cognition of disclosure toward a performative recognition which itself appears torn between the involuntary demands of law's (re)union and a relation-making giving (up) of the self that seems to exceed the grasp of judgment. Faced with this dynamic and the problem of whether the confession holds the potential to hold perpetrators accountable, the discourse of transitional justice has tended to reply in one of three ways. The first and most influential response is that the confession turns the perpetrator into a recognizable liberal subject, a figure whose expression recognizes the rule of law and seeks standing before it, the ground needed to request recognition's provision(s). This

[17]Foucault, *Hermeneutics* 365; Foucault, *Politics* 195. The differences are subtle, particularly as the latter is tied to the learning that energizes *parrhēsia*, a training in truth-telling and the "frankness, freedom and openness that leads one to say what one has to say, as one wishes to say it, when one wishes to say it, and in the form one thinks is necessary for saying it" (Foucault, *Hermeneutics* 372, 377). Also see Tell ("Rhetoric").

[18]Through Hegel, Bernstein offers one view of such an *ethos* ("Confession" 54–60).

transformative work need not be limited to the courtroom, a fact that is made clear by the way in which many truth commissions warrant their work on law-making grounds. As Ruti Teitel would have it, the confession is woven into (and by) "legal rituals" and "social knowledge" that "make for transitional historical accountability," a process that is given—from the start—to a "liberalizing political change" that amounts to the assumption (we cannot say transition here) of the "liberal political identity" deemed necessary for "political unity" (*Transitional* 71, 225). Yet, even as the confession's performance is dedicated to instantiating and supporting the rule of law, a rule that is claimed to precede the confession, the latter's performativity may betray that the former's integrity cannot be presupposed absent a critique of its violence. This possibility has largely escaped transitional justice discourse. Indeed, the mainstream case for confession grapples little if at all with the problem of legal violence, the atrocities and violations that are undertaken in the law's name and sanctioned by its power, not least a logic of exception in which legal violence is held out as a necessary way of preserving the legal order and its promise of justice (Esmeir 1545). In such circumstances, the confession may offer little more than an opportunity for perpetrators to cling to the legality of their actions and imbue them with a "prior" accountability that can be questioned only at the risk of upsetting the law's continuity. When this tactic is generalized, when it is rendered a *topos*, the presumption that the confession's work is given to promoting the recognition of law's rule may well solve the problem of legal violence. But it does so only by dismantling legal violence as a problem and abandoning altogether the question of whether rule of law's integrity hinges on a critical inquiry into its rule of recognition, the contingent historical-political norms that delineate the law's power and which the law itself cannot define.

In a second account, one that is not without an echo of law, the discourse of transitional justice casts the confession as a way to (re)turn the public-deliberative subject. As it sacrifices the expressed justifications that have funded conflict, the confession troubles if not topples the principle of identity, the internalized grammar that conditions the subject's value on the necessity of (its) violence. The relinquishment of these commitments—in general and in particular—marks a demonstration of good faith, a (re)turn to the work of securing civic trust and defining the collective interest. The difficulty, however, is that the deliberative conventions deemed to enable public life, if they exist at all in the aftermath of protracted conflict and systematic abuse, may underwrite or pre-script the confession such that its performative quality is easily reduced to stage(d) work which both provokes the charge of insincerity and leads perpetrators to claim that they have been led blindly into a punitive-disciplinary alley.[19] Recalling Foucault, the larger underlying problem here is the way the confession is (pre)defined as a narrative (re)making of public subjects. Even as such a project aims to dissolve the

[19]On this dynamic set into the context of transitional justice, see Salazar.

identity-based roots of conflict—a tremendous problem in the scenes to which transitional justice is called—it may hail a multicultural citizen whose oath to unity *as* difference yields the very identitarian logic that the confession's promise of unity *in* difference is pledged to oppose.

The third view holds that the confession turns its subject from instrumental actor to a participant in the development of intersubjective understanding between individuals, not least victims and perpetrators. Here, the confession's recognition is figured as a turn from an "eye for eye" to an "I for an I." Thus, when I confess, when I reply that it *was* me, this "I" is composed through my saying "I" at the same time that its meaning is wrested away, given away to an other on whom I depend, not least for a response that cannot be requested.[20] This work leaves Barthes to worry after the exhaustion of language itself. For his part, Derrida senses a welcome to the machine; committed to giving myself away in the name of being accountable to (and for) an other, "I" am able to say the "I" that interrupts "me" only as the confession is rendered commonplace, a performance whose terms have arrived too early and, as such, too late. As the "I" that "I" offer is never and always behind its words, to recall Barthes once more, "the subject of the speech-act can never be the same as the one who acted yesterday: the *I* of the discourse can no longer be the site where a previously stored up person is innocently restored" (17). The confession's turn is a turn back, away from the moment to which it is given.

With these three scenarios, the discourse of transitional justice variously envisions confession's defining turn. Considered closely, however, this movement appears more complex, a (re)turning (re)turn in which the confession moves back and forth across the word's course of re-cognition and a course of recognizing words. More precisely, the disclosure of past deeds given to naming an unnamable truth *and* the ambiguous self-sacrificing expression that manifests guilt, culpability, complicity, and perhaps regret, remorse, and restoration abide in a (non)relation. This undecidable connection is a movement of potential and a potential movement, a shuttling within and between an enabling (un)speak-ability and an energizing (non)account-ability. Thus, as a submission of words and a submission to words no longer one's own and as the confession's respective movements variously point toward, support, and undercut one another, its speech action beckons the question of irresponsibility. It presents the question of whether and how the confession's turn evades and ultimately denigrates its own promise, an embodied expression of truth that sheds the pretence of appearance in name of coming to terms. All too well, we know the charge that follows, the rage against hypocrisy that unfurls from even an intuition of the confession's deception: its words do not match its deeds, in any sense. Neither the aura of confession's spontaneous expression nor the rigors of its institutional prescription can dispel doubts about its interest and motivation.

[20]This position proceeds under the influence of Émile Benveniste. For further discussion set in the context of the confession, see Barthes and Sanders 159–161.

In transition, in a moment of becoming that lays tremendous stress on the need for words to be real, the confession's turn rings hollow if not duplicitous. The confession offers an impossible sincerity, impossible for the way it obscures its own lack of standing and fails to assume the risk carried in its expression.

So, the confession is not what it seems. And, as they resound with a call for justice, the words of testimony deserve more (and less) than the hypocrisy that abides in the confession's movement and signals its irresponsibility. We grasp this, by the fraught terms of human rights discourse, by law, and perhaps—if only ironically—by heart.[21] Yet, without relinquishing the ambivalence about what was never said, consider Heidegger in 1943: "The answer to the question of the essence of truth is the saying of a turning with the history of Being" (154). Here, for now, there appears another turn, a turning of the confession's irresponsibility toward the question of its (ir)response-ability. Beyond its disclosure and its account, does the confession hold the capacity for a response, an (im)potential of turning (with) words that precisely recalls how recognition was grasped in antiquity as discovery, a "turning right about" that unfolds in the experience of language as such, in the experience of the "saying of a turning?"[22] If so, such expression neither figures nor abandons duty, a demand that the confession respond in one way, another, or not at all. Rather, it remains a question, an asking *after* (an inquiring of, a subsequent interrogative of) the word's turn while standing in its midst. Not then a decision to give up language but an experience of language as a question itself, a struggle with language's (in)operativity, the turning turn from within which it offers itself up and conserves itself—for itself. (Ir)response-ability then as the question of the (im)potentiality of a response, an expression that sounds an echo of prophecy, before the prophetic expression (*khrēsmos)* was converted from the announcement of a choice in terms not our own to the compulsion of apocalyptic prediction.[23] Neither the confession nor the confessor offer the true word or the word's truth. Rather, there is a question—for us. There is an unwelcome question. Impertinent, at the very best, as it is a reply to the question "Was it you?," the confession asks how to turn with(in) language in its turning, a movement that is not ours but which we appropriate in the name of what Benjamin named "mythic violence," the very violence that confession is called on to disclose and abandon. What response then to the confession's (ir)response-ability? With this question, as a question, it becomes easier to appreciate Butler's passing but crucial claim that the confession betrays the "priority of rhetoric to ethics" (Butler *Giving* 134) and how it may call the discourse of transitional justice to the work of language itself, to an inquiry into the unstable conditions of

[21]This refers, of course, to Arendt's crucial discussion of hypocrisy in *On Revolution.*

[22]Elsewhere, I have offered a fuller reflection on this dynamic in relation to hypocrisy's "role" in human rights discourse ("Rhetorical Question of Human Rights").

[23]If we blame Heidegger, this blame may have roots in his turning away from the former in favor of the latter.

undertaking response that does not forsake an attentiveness to the experience of language as not (a) given, an experience of the struggle over what must be said in a moment when we cannot know what to say.

It may be possible to speak of there being no certain grounds for expression not as a prologue to leveling hypocrisy with a righteousness that terrorizes its own words, but as a question of the (im)position with which we come to the word's violence, a violence that appears in the confession and which it cannot transcend (and indeed may perform) save through an appeal to a law of endless exception, a fate that allows the confession to covertly establish the ground and then the permission to submit a concluding and perhaps pernicious question of its own—*Will you forgive me?*[24] This troublesome positioning well explains the hostility to the confession's appearance in testimony's orbit, a justified antipathy that nevertheless carries a risk of its own: the forbidding of questions, not least of the costs to victims that accrue when testimony is conditioned on the assumption of *homo narrans*. This is partly to say that if it is to address, let alone redress, barbarism, the confessional gesture supported by transitional justice discourse may offer a (re)turn only as it bears witness to the way in which the rule of its law may deter discovery, an inquiry that asks after the (ir)response-ability on which the groundless beginning of transition may depend. Furthermore, at a larger level, at the level of human rights, the rhetorical question of confession may offer a way to both agree with and respond to David Kennedy's insight that human rights institutions tend to focus less on "enabling a discussion of what it means to be human, of who is human, of how humans might relate to one another" than developing a "knowledge about the shape of emancipation" that "crushes this discussion under the weight of moral condemnation, legal adjudication, textual certainty, and political power" (14).[25] Certainly this contention can be read as the starting point of an "excuse," a logic that would somehow excuse evil. What complicates this conclusion, however, is the possibility that the long fashionable split between theory and practice in human rights discourse has legitimized the priority of "engagement" at the expense of questioning the costs of its attending piety, a sacred commitment to a discourse that remains altogether reluctant to confess its lack of interest in the making of (its) discourse as such.

References

Agamben, Giorgio. *Remnants of Auschwitz: The Witness and the Archive.* Trans. Daniel Heller-Roazen. New York: Zone Books, 2000. Print.

Arendt, Hannah. *Eichmann in Jerusalem.* New York: Penguin Books, 1963/1994. Print.

[24]See Krog. With respect to the ensuing question of forgiveness, I have addressed this elsewhere at some length ("A Question of Forgiving Words").

[25]With respect to the problem of what is involved in "making claims" within human rights discourse and the costs of the pragmatism that operates as a trump in human rights discourse, see Butler ("Afterword").

———. *On Revolution.* New York: Viking Press, 1965. Print.

Arendt, Hannah. "Truth and Politics." *Between Past and Future.* New York: Penguin Books, 1977. 227–264. Print.

Barthes, Roland. "To Write: An Intransitive Verb?" *The Rustle of Language.* Trans. Richard Howard. Berkeley: University of California Press, 1989. 11–21. Print.

Benveniste, Émile. *Problems in General Linguistics.* Trans. Mary Meek. Coral Cables, FL: University of Miami Press, 1971. Print.

Bernard-Donals, Michael and Richard Glejzer. *Witnessing the Disaster: Essays on Representation and the Holocaust.* Madison: University of Wisconsin Press, 2003. Print.

Bernstein, J. M. "Confession and Forgiveness: Hegel's Poetics of Action." *Beyond Representation: Philosophy and Poetic Imagination.* Ed. Richard Eldridge. Cambridge: Cambridge University Press, 1996. 34–65. Print.

———. "Bare Life, Bearing Witness: Auschwitz and the Pornography of Horror." *Parallax* 10.1 (2004): 2–16. Print.

Blanchot, Maurice. *The Writing of the Disaster.* Trans. Ann Smock. Lincoln: University of Nebraska Press, 1995. Print.

Butler, Judith. *Giving an Account of Oneself.* New York: Fordham University Press, 2007. Print.

———. "Afterword." *PMLA* 121.5 (2006): 1658–1661. Print.

Cole, Catherine. *Performing South Africa's Truth Commission.* Bloomington: Indiana University Press, 2010. Print.

de Man, Paul. "Excuses (Confessions)." *Allegories of Reading.* New Haven, CT: Yale University Press, 1979. 278–302. Print.

Derrida, Jacques. "History of the Lie: Prolegomena." *Without Alibi.* Trans. Peggy Kamuf. Palo Alto: Stanford University Press, 2002. 28–70. Print.

———. "Typewriter Ribbon: Limited Inc (2)." *Without Alibi.* Trans. Peggy Kamuf. Palo Alto: Stanford University Press, 2002. 71–160. Print.

———. "The University without Condition." *Without Alibi.* Trans. Peggy Kamuf. Palo Alto: Stanford University Press, 2002. 202–237. Print.

Doxtader, Erik. "The Rhetorical Question of Human Rights—A Preface." *Quarterly Journal of Speech* 96.4 (2010): 353–379. Print.

———. "A Question of Forgiving Words." *Public Forgiveness.* Ed. Bas van Stockom. Forthcoming 2012. Available on request.

Elster, Jon. *Closing the Books: Transitional Justice in Historical Perspective.* New York: Cambridge University Press, 2004. Print.

Esmeir, Samera. "On Making Dehumanization Possible." *PMLA* 125.5 (2006): 1544–1552. Print.

Felman, Shoshana and Dori Laub. *Testimony: Crises of Witnessing in Literature, Psychoanalysis, and History.* New York: Routledge, 1992. Print.

Foucault, Michel. *The History of Sexuality: An Introduction.* Volume 1. Trans. Robert Hurley. New York: Vintage, 1990. Print.

———. *The Politics of Truth.* Ed. Sylvere Lotringer. Cambridge: Semiotext(e), 1997. Print.

———. *Aesthetics: Essential Works of Foucault.* Ed. James Faubion. New York: Penguin, 2000. Print.

———. "Truth and Juridical Forms." *Power: Essential Works of Michel Foucault, 1954–1984.* Ed. James Faubion. New York: The New Press, 2000. 1–89. Print.

———. *The Hermeneutics of the Subject: Lectures at the College de France, 1981–1982.* Trans. Graham Burchell. New York: Palgrave, 2005. Print.

Foster, Don, Paul, Haupt, and Marésa de Beer. *The Theatre of Violence: Narratives of protagonists in the South African conflict.* Johannesburg: HRSC Press, 2005. Print.

Friedlander, Saul. Ed. *Probing the Limits of Representation: Nazism and the "Final Solution."* Cambridge: Harvard University Press, 1992. Print.

Haidu, Peter. "The Dialectics of Unspeakability: Language, Silence and the Narratives of Desubjectification." *Probing the Limits of Representation: Nazism and the "Final Solution."* Ed. Saul Friedlander. Cambridge: Harvard University Press, 1992. Print.

Hayner, Priscilla. *Unspeakable Truths: Transitional Justice and the Challenge of Truth Commissions.* New York: Routledge, 2010. Print.

Heidegger, Martin. "On The Essence of Truth." *Pathmarks.* Ed. William McNeill. Trans. John Sallis. Cambridge: Cambridge University Press, 1998. Print.

Kennedy, David. *The Dark Side of Virtue: Reassessing International Humanitarianism.* Princeton, NJ: Princeton University Press, 2004. Print.

Krog, Antjie. *Country of my Skull: Guilt, Sorrow and the Limits of Forgiveness in the New South Africa.* New York: Times Books, 1998. Print.

Lanzmann, Claude. "The Obscenity of Understanding: An Evening with Claude Lanzmann." *Trauma: Explorations in Memory.* Ed. Cathy Caruth. Baltimore: Johns Hopkins University Press, 1995. 200–219. Print.

Mandel, Naomi. *Against the Unspeakable: Complicity, the Holocaust and Slavery in America.* Charlottesville: University of Virginia Press, 2006. Print.

Moon, Claire. *Narrating Political Reconciliation: South Africa's Truth and Reconciliation Commission.* New York: Lexington Books, 2008. Print.

Payne, Leigh. *Unsettling Accounts: Neither Truth nor Reconciliation in Confessions of State Violence.* Durham, NC: Duke University Press, 2007. Print.

Report of the Office of the High Commissioner for Human Rights. "Implementation of General Assembly Resolution 60/251 of 15 March 2006 Entitled 'Human Rights Council'—Right to Truth." (A/HRC/5/7). 7 June 2007, 16. Print.

Ross, Fiona C. *Bearing Witness: Women and the Truth and Reconciliation Commission in South Africa.* London: Pluto Press, 2003. Print.

Rotberg, Robert and Dennis Thompson, eds. *Truth v. Justice: The Morality of Truth Commissions.* Princeton, NJ: Princeton University Press, 2000. Print.

Salazar, Philippe. *An African Athens: Rhetoric and the Shaping of Democracy in South Africa.* London: Laurence Erlbaum, 2002. Print.

Sanders, Mark. *Ambiguities of Witnessing: Law and Literature in the Time of a Truth Commission.* Palo Alto, CA: Stanford University Press, 2009. Print.

Smith, James. *Speech and Theology: Language and the Logic of Incarnation.* New York: Routledge, 2002. Print.

Taylor, Chloe. *The Culture of Confession from Augustine to Foucault: A Genealogy of the 'Confessing Animal'.* New York: Routledge, 2008. Print.

Teitel, Ruti. *Transitional Justice.* Oxford: Oxford University Press, 2000. Print.

———. "Transitional Justice Genealogy." *Harvard Human Rights Journal* 16 (2003): 69–94. Print.

Tell, Dave. "Beyond Mnemotechnics: Confession and Memory in Augustine." *Philosophy & Rhetoric* 39.3 (2006): 233–253. Print.

———. "Rhetoric and Power: An Inquiry into Foucault's Critique of Confession." *Philosophy & Rhetoric* 43.2 (2010): 95–117. Print.

Truth and Reconciliation Commission. *Truth and Reconciliation Commission of South Africa Report.* 7 Vols. Cape Town: Juta, 1998/2003. Print.

Villa-Vicencio, Charles. *Walk with Us and Listen: Political Reconciliation in Africa.* Washington DC: Georgetown University Press, 2010. Print.

Human Rights Rhetoric of Recognition

Wendy S. Hesford

Through her reading of the editors' introduction and ensuing four essays, Hesford approaches human rights as a discourse of public persuasion that envisions certain scenes of sociopolitical recognition, normative notions of subject formation, and paradoxical particularities. She joins contributors in their interrogation of the normative scenes of sociopolitical recognition on which the human rights paradox of exclusive universalism rests. Yet, she also maintains that in our efforts to construe a more inclusive human rights history that we are mindful of distinctions between the rhetorical tactics of individuals and social movements and differences of geopolitical scale and scope.

Who is represented in the history of human rights? Whose struggles speak through human rights history and rhetoric? A rhetorical orientation to the history of human rights consistent with the editorial framework of this special issue suggests an emphasis on human rights history as *authorship* (Baxi 184). From this vantage point, as legal scholar Upendra Baxi puts it, the "universality of human rights ceases to be an *abstract* idea [. . .] and becomes a *living* practice" (21, emphasis in original). To approach human rights as a living practice is to view human rights as a cultural system and to envision culture as contentious, as "unbounded, contested, and connected to relations of power" (Merry 15). Furthermore, to approach the history of human rights as a struggle over meaning is to disrupt myopic narratives and to reveal the rhetorical mechanisms of assemblage, classification, and categorization that structure this history and its translation into cultural forms.

In focusing on human rights rhetoric, the editors draw our attention to "how rights are represented in language and symbolism, how advocates construct particular responses in contingent situations, and how public debates influence communities, interpretations of rights, and rights enforcement" (204). Contributors newly narrate human rights history, expanding the scenes of historical recognition by recalibrating who and what qualifies as a subject of human rights past and future, and deepening our grasp of the ideological journeys of the concept of universal human rights and its fundamental paradoxes. Two recognition scenes emerge as central to contributors' arguments and as a product of the historigraphic dimensions of their work: historical recognition scenes that aim to integrate formally excluded subjects into human rights history, and embedded scenes of rhetorical address that function as evidence of the human rights paradox of exclusive universalism and imagine an ethics of responsibility that moves beyond notions of subjectivity, agency, and recognition founded on subjection.

Human rights history has been dominated by antagonistic struggles for recognition tethered to the Hegelian dialectic of the self–other. Throughout the history of human rights certain bodies have been attributed the status of "fully" human beings; slaves, colonized peoples, indigenous peoples, women, children, and the "insane" marked as Other and therefore as not fully human were by definition not "considered worthy of being bearers of human rights" (Baxi 44). Not only is there a long history of exclusive universalism in Western philosophy, rhetoric, and law, but rights talk is limited in its ability to address the structural violence and symbolic mechanisms that have functioned as modalities of subordination and exclusion, such as normative identity categories (Brown 52–70). Moreover, given that human rights norms are identified with political democracy, the rights that are privileged in international politics are those "that strengthen, legitimize, and export the liberal democratic state to non-Western societies" (Mutua 215). For example, under the Bush administration, U.S. military interventions in Afghanistan and Iraq were staged as gift-giving human rights recognition scenes. Yet it is not enough to simply become aware of the paradox of human rights' exclusive universalism and the imperatives of empire gift-wrapped in a messianic human rights rhetoric (Hesford and Kozol). As contributors propose, we need to interrogate the normative scenes of sociopolitical recognition on which the paradox of exclusive universalism rests and the role of the humanities in perpetuating these norms (see Hesford).[1]

Contingent Identities

Human rights might be understood as a discourse of public persuasion that envisions certain scenes of sociopolitical recognition, normative notions of subject formation, and paradoxical particularities. The 1948 Universal Declaration of Human Rights (UDHR), often considered the spiritual parent of international human

[1]The dramatic term *scene* here implies a rhetorical configuration that is both spatial and temporal and yet contingent. My use of the term invokes Slaughter's usage in *Human Rights Inc.*, in which he describes (self)-recognition scenes as "the moment of personification (or incorporation) when the individual becomes conscious of being a subject to and for the rules of law and narrative." For Slaughter, a recognition scene is also, however, "a moment when [. . .] the newly incorporated citizen-subject becomes aware of 'the right [of everyone] to recognition everywhere as a person before the law' " (UDHR) (254).

rights law, confers universal personhood upon every human being, but it implies that this recognition—the incorporation of the subject into the regime of rights—has yet to be attained. First, the declaration assumes an a priori universal subject that both preexists and comes into being—that, in Joseph Slaughter's words, "becom[es] what [it] already is by right" ("Enabling Fictions" 1415). It is particularly important to consider this narrative of legal personhood because the sociopolitical process of recognition that it relies on often reiterates social hierarchies, especially when privileged groups and powerful nations are configured as the distributors of rights for those unable to claim them. Contributors interrogate these social hierarchies and dialectical self–other scenes of rhetorical address by exposing the relationship between sociopolitical recognition and ideological subjection, and several contributors provide powerful examples of cultural productions (public addresses, street protests and performances, documentary photographs, and theoretical musings) that re-imagine this relationship in ways that seek a mutual recognition—reciprocity configured through rhetorical constructs of witnessing—or question the norms that structure the politics of recognition and its hierarchical dynamics of privilege and domination (Oliver 23–50).

In "A Question of Confession's Discovery," Erik Doxtader contemplates the scenes of sociopolitical and legal recognition that characterize the transitional justice movement, specifically truth commissions that solicit perpetrators' confessions in an attempt to fill in the historical record and carry out victims' "right to truth" (269). Doxtader observes that "the confession's performance offers . . . a a turn from violent division to an abiding unity in difference" (270–71). But, as he also points out, the promise of public truth-telling and healing that perpetrators' confessions are purported to enable also comes with risk; the confession, that is, "displac[es] the witness's own voice," (267) "overshadows the experience of victims, blurs the difference between guilt and trauma, weakens the drive for prosecutions, and dilutes collective moral outrage" (269). Doxtader thus exposes the perverse exception that is staged through the truth commission's broadening of the scenes of sociopolitical recognition, wherein perpetrators' accounts of acts "offer little more than an opportunity for perpetrators to cling to the legality of their actions and imbue them with a 'prior' accountability that can be questioned only at the risk of upsetting the law's continuity" (276). Doxtader's analysis of these fraught confessions and scenes of misrecognition reveals that the incorporation of the individual into the human rights system is not simply a process of attribution; all acts of self- and social recognition are contingent and involve identity negotiations and changes in subjectivity, which for survivors often involves taking on a double-subjectivity as rights-bearer and victim (Merry 181) and revisiting the trauma of violation by bearing witness to perpetrators' staged confessions. Despite the ideal of mutual recognition that inspires truth and reconciliation efforts, Doxtader shows that human rights institutions operate in a dialectical economy of recognition that perpetuate the subject/other-object dichotomy. Yet in foregrounding the contingencies that re/produce these relationships, he also demonstrates the value of a rhetorically based approach to human rights formations of ethical responsibility and justice. Baxi sums up these contingencies well: "The bearer of universal human rights is . . . no individual human being or community with a pre-posited 'essence' but a being born with a right to invent practices of identification, contest identities pre-formed by tradition, and the power to negotiate subversive subject-positions . . . . [T]he bearers of human rights remain *contingent persons*" (149).

Cindy Patton's focus on the recent shifts in international AIDS policy and activism reveals the contingent identities that different conceptions of rights compel. In "Rights Language and HIV Treatment: Universal Care or Population Control?," Patton notes that early WHO rights-talk, developed with persons with AIDS (PWA) and their advocacy groups (251), conjoined the discourses of international human rights and U.S. civil rights. Recently, the WHO has taken a new approach—treatment-as-prevention—developed by demographers and epidemiologists (252). The turn from the rights of PWAs to the rights of populations to be free of the virus, Patton argues, "transformed the actual once-speaking bodies of persons living with AIDS into 'vulnerable groups' embedded in a larger population, where they experience loss of rights and an inability to articulate wrongs" (255). She continues, arguing that this change "affects the ability to make claims: a population cannot meaningfully be said to 'suffer,' and yet contemporary calls to be better global citizens are founded directly on the articulation of individual human suffering" (264). These approaches represent "two ontologically incommensurable forms of witnessing that underwrite the different forms of rights" (255): *witnessing illness* (an embodied witnessing that attends to the subject and enforceable rights) and *witnessing disease* ("the observation of the epidemic from the point of view of those who imagine themselves not subject to the disease, a disembodied meta-vision" [255]). Patton upholds a view of legal personhood predicated on the normative identity of the victim in her focus of the rights of wronged bodies. Her appeal to embodied witnessing is less symptomatic of human rights attachment to trauma and injury, however, than it is indicative of human rights advocates and scholars need to consider what is at stake, and for whom, in the disinvestment of human rights' attachment to an identity-based paradigm of recognition.

Contingent Histories

In "Human Rights and Civil Rights: The Advocacy and Activism of African-American Women Writers," Jacqueline Jones Royster and Molly Cochran articulate the overlapping "discourse horizons" of U.S. civil rights activism and global human rights activism (214). Their revisionary project contributes to goals associated with the "contemporary" human rights paradigm. According to Baxi, in contrast to the "modern" human rights paradigm and its exclusionary criteria (the tradition of rights-talk and the philosophy of natural law that emerged from the American and

French Revolutions), the "contemporary" human rights paradigm (rights positivized in international law in the period following the Second World War) is based on the principle of inclusion (42). In his rejection of the Eurocentric "narrative monopoly" on the history of human rights (40), Baxi opts, as do Royster and Cochran, for an "intercultural... discourse on the genealogy of human rights" (39), which encompasses social movements, such as civil rights, women's rights, indigenous rights, gay rights, refugee rights, and, disability rights.

Royster and Cochran argue that African-American women writer/activists "have defined themselves by their humanity, their human dignity, and their rights to justice, equality, and empowerment within the human enterprise" (218). The rhetorical visions of nineteenth-century writer/activists, such as Maria W. Stewart, Frances Ellen Watkins Harper, and Ida B. Wells-Barnett, who extended their critique of slavery to broader appeals for liberty and equality for all and twentieth-century writer/activists, such as Mary Church Terrell and June Jordan, perform an evidentiary function in the authors' call for an inclusive human rights history and an expansion of its canonical figures and texts (219–20). Royster and Cochran's emphasis on the concept of human dignity might give us pause, given the actions the conflation of these terms in U.S. foreign policy has been used to legitimate, especially the post-9/11 policies of the Bush administration, which have proven to be antithetical to human rights visions. Under the Bush administration, the more amorphous *human dignity* replaced *human rights* as the policy term of choice—a rhetoric that complemented and helped to legitimize the administration's appeals to military action grounded in humanitarian and faith-based initiatives rather than in international human rights law (Mertus 379). Royster and Cochran observe the spiritual grounding of African-American civil rights writer/activists' invocations of the concept of human dignity; yet they also demonstrate how these women's contributions went "beyond spirituality and Christian morality to establish [rhetorical] traditions of social, economic, and political critique" (218).

In 1893, Wells-Barnett delivered a speech in which she rallied against the Republican Party, who was silent in the face of the terrorism of lynching: "I long with all the intensity of my soul for... this nation to demand that from Greenland's icy mountains to the coral reefs of the Southern seas, mob rule shall be put down and equal and exact justice be accorded to every citizen of whatever race, who finds a home within the borders of the land of the free and the home of the brave" (220). Here, Wells-Barnett attests to the hypocrisy between our nation's founding principles and its practices, forecasting what would become known as the fundamental paradox of international human rights law, namely its dependency on the sovereignty of nation-states for its implementation. Notably, Royster and Cochran attend to the internal incongruities between civil rights and human rights in the context of resurgent American nationalism and exceptionalism. For example, dominant depictions of civil rights violations as "vexing mis-alignments within an otherwise normal national landscape" fostered national denial narratives that cast "[c]ivil rights activism . . . [as] an aberration that we would just have go graciously unnoticed" (216–17). The discourse of American exceptionalism has and continues to safeguard such narratives by diverting attention from the human rights violations that occur within the United States to those that occur outside of its national borders.

In "'From the Eye to the Soul': Industrial Labor's Mary Harris 'Mother' Jones and the Rhetorics of Display," Mari Boor Tonn examines Jones's "legendary" rhetorical prowess as a union agitator and advocate for federal labor reforms (236). She traces Jones's "fifty-year crusade in making the nation 'see' class injustice" and her faith in photographic realism in "nourishing moral action" (235). As Jones once said, "scribbling has no effect on the public mind. If you *show* . . . real real evil and wake up the sleepy, indifferent public, you will get these conditions changed" (quoted in Tonn, 236). Through her activist displays of documentary photographs depicting the exploitation of miners and class injustices, Jones spotlighted the atrocities of the Colorado Coalfield War of 1913–1914, which consisted of 1,200 striking mining families living in "improvised ghettos" outside of Ludlow (233). Striking miners and their families endured political intimidation, government surveillance, random sniper fire, beatings, and the suspension of habeas corpus and civil courts (233). In the end, the Coalfield War "claimed nearly seventy lives with exponentially many more wounded," and as Tonn notes, this was "but a sliver of several hundred annual Colorado mining casualties" (234).

The Colorado Coalfield War galvanized public attention largely because of the "multitude of photographs recording for all to 'see' the gilded-age industry's iron fist" (234). Tonn argues that the U.S. industrial labor movement was "[a]mong the first U.S. social movements to exploit myriad forms of rhetorical display in championing human rights protections," suggesting that it "contributed to expanding, elevating, and accelerating consideration of human rights to a global imperative unfolding following World War I and eventually codified in the 1948 United Nations' Universal Declaration on Human Rights" (232). Tonn provides plenty of evidence of Jones's rhetorical dexterity in advancing federal labor rights and the U.S. government's and the mining industry's violations against miners and their families. But there is less evidence that suggests that these early labor struggles displayed an international human rights conscience that prioritized the concept of rights as interdependent and indivisible. Indeed, Tonn provides copious evidence to comprehend better the nationalist parameters of these early labor struggles and Jones's advocacy tactics. For example, Tonn cites a speech that Jones gave at a congressional hearing just three days after the Ludlow arson. Here Jones exhibits a materialist rhetoric of class injustice and class warfare in making her argument for government ownership of the mines. Jones calls forth a communal obligation that has more affinity with Marxist critiques than with the liberal individualism of human rights.

I draw these distinctions not to quarantine domestic human rights appeals and activism or solidify a separate conceptual sphere for economic rights. Clearly, human rights include civil, political, social, economic, and cultural rights. Clearly, rights discourses intersect. And undoubtedly, the contemporary human rights movement and earlier social movements share rhetorical tactics of exposure and shaming, and a realist documentary aesthetic. As rhetorical critics, we are likely to recognize these convergences, but in so doing we should not ignore differences of scale between social movements that focus on the rights of citizens in a resolutely national framework and the development of an international human rights movement, characterized by the concept of *universal* rights and the proliferation of transnational governmental and nongovernmental human rights institutions, and international human rights instruments and laws.

Single-cause movements may have contributed to the creation of a culture of public engagement, but as the historian Resa Afshari's suggests, it was only when single-cause movements began to articulate interconnections among causes that the idea of *universal* human rights took hold (34–35).[2] Afshari acknowledges the historical significance of social movements such as the anti-slavery and abolitionist movements, labor movements, and anti-imperialist movements, among others, but he makes a persuasive case for their qualified influence in the development of the concept of *universal* human rights and the international human rights movement.[3] For example, Afshari claims that the "autonomous labor movement remained largely a single-causal movement" (32):

> From its inception the labor movement became imbedded in the racist culture of the country and remained as such before, during and after the Civil War—in fact, well into the twentieth century.... After the Civil War, only in rare occasion and largely for tactical reasons did white labor organizations willingly admit black workers—in segregated units.... Despite its widespread claims for advancing human rights, the Marxist left associated with labor became

[2]Afshari also exposes the contradictions in the discourses and actions of prominent individuals in single-issue struggles in order to further demonstrate the unfeasibility of an unencumbered progress narrative for the development of human rights. To make his case, Afshari looks to figures such as William Lloyd Garrison, whose notion of "Universal Emancipation" and whose vision of Perfectionism anchored in evangelical millenarianism was antithetical to the pragmatic principles found in human rights discourse during the next century (18–19). In contrast to white abolitionists who saw themselves as the distributors of rights, John Brown's activism rose above many of the racist attitudes of the time, as shown by his endorsement of "black people acting as the human agents of their own liberation" (20). Nevertheless, as Afshari notes, Brown's attitude toward other issues, such as a strictly enforced morality, were not conducive to a human rights vision (21).

[3]Afshari's critique of these linkages appears in a work in which he is also highly critical of histories that locate the origins of human rights in pre-modern, ancient philosophers and prophets and argue that the moral vision of human rights belongs to no particular civilization (3). He insists that scholars recognize the key differences between pre-modern notions of justice and duty and contemporary notions of universal human rights (6). "The notion of 'inherent rights simply by virtue of being human beings' belongs to the post-enlightenment humanity" (8). Similarly, Samuel Moyn criticizes human rights scholars that "wander backward—disinclined to face up to the recent vintage and contingent beginnings of their subject" (7).

> profoundly communitarian and illiberal, creating a long term obstacle for the emergence of a human rights culture. (32–34)

The methodological challenge that has plagued historiographers and rhetorical critics alike lies not in the pursuit of an inclusive human rights history, but in our insufficient attention to distinctions of geopolitical scale and scope, distinctions between the rhetorical tactics of individuals and the momentum of a social movement, and the contradictory subjectivities that human rights law, and, more broadly, rights-talk compels. Contributors to this special issue stage these methodological challenges as scenes of (mis)recognition in foregrounding the contingencies that shape human rights appeals and that foster the emergence or destruction of human rights contexts and the incessant dual between human rights' global aspirations and nationalist retorts.

References

Afshari, Reza. "On Historiography of Human Rights: Reflections on Paul Gordon Lauren's The Evolution of International Human Rights: Visions Seen." *Human Rights Quarterly* 29.1 (2007): 1–67. Print.

Baxi, Upendra. *The Future of Human Rights.* 2nd ed. New Delhi: Oxford University Press, 2006. Print.

Brown, Wendy. *States of Injury: Power and Freedom in Late Modernity.* Princeton, NJ: Princeton University Press, 1995. Print.

Hesford, Wendy S. *Spectacular Rhetorics: Human Rights Visions, Recognitions, Feminisms.* Durham: Duke University Press, 2011. Print.

Hesford, Wendy S. and Wendy Kozol, eds. "Introduction." *Just Advocacy? Women's Human Rights, Transnational Feminisms, and the Politics of Representation.* New Brunswick, NJ: Rutgers University Press, 2005. 1–29. Print.

Merry, Sally Engle. *Human Rights and Gender Violence: Translating International Law into Local Justice.* Chicago: University of Chicago Press, 2006. Print.

Mertus, Julie. "The New U.S. Human Rights Policy: A Radical Departure." *International Studies Perspectives* 4.4 (2003): 371–384. Print.

Moyn, Samuel. "On the Genealogy of Morals." *The Nation.* 16 April 2007: 25–31. Print.

Mutua, Makau. "Savages, Victims, and Saviors: The Metaphor of Human Rights." *Harvard International Law Journal* 42 (2001): 201–245. Print.

Oliver, Kelly. *Witnessing beyond Recognition.* Minneapolis: University of Minnesota Press, 2001. Print.

Slaughter, Joseph R. "Enabling Fictions and Novel Subjects: The *Bildungs-roman* and International Human Rights Law." *PMLA* 121.5 (2006): 1405–1424. Print.

———. *Human Rights, Inc.: The World Novel, Narrative Form, and International Law.* New York: Fordham University Press, 2007. Print.

A Visual Sequence

Human Rights Rhetoric

Lester C. Olson & Arabella Lyon

Statues portray "Freedom from Want" and "Freedom of Speech" for a United Nations exhibit by the Office of War Information in Rockefeller Plaza, New York, N.Y. This exhibit featured a copy of the Atlantic charter, with amplifiers at each end broadcasting speeches by Franklin D. Roosevelt, Winston Churchill, and Chiang Kai-Shek every half hour, and surrounded by statues of the four freedoms. Segment from a larger photograph by Marjory Collins, March 1943. Courtesy of the Prints and Photographs Division of the Library of Congress and Flickr.com. (Retrieve from http://www.loc.gov/pictures/collection/fsac/item/fsa1992001537/PP/ or http://www.flickr.com/photos/library_of_congress/2179127293/.)

"Handicapped!" This women's suffrage poster by the Artists' Suffrage League features a woman in a row-boat, struggling in high waves, while a man relaxes on a sailboat with a sail labeled "votes." Westminster Palace can be seen in the background. Four color poster printed by Carl Hentschel Ltd., 182, 183 & 184 Fleet Street, E.C., London, UK. Circa 1910–1919. Courtesy of the Prints and Photographs Division of the Library of Congress and WikiMedia Commons. (Retrieve from: http://commons.wikimedia.org/wiki/File:Handicapped!_Women%27s_suffrage_poster,_1910s.jpg.)

First grade children, some of Japanese-American ancestry, at the Weill public school in San Francisco, California pledge allegiance to the flag of the United States. The evacuees of Japanese ancestry will be interned in war relocation authority centers for the duration of the war. Farm Security Administration and Office of War Information Photograph, attributed to Dorothea Lange, April 1942. Courtesy of the Prints and Photographs Division of the Library of Congress and WikiMedia Commons. (Retrieve from: https://secure.wikimedia.org/wikipedia/commons/wiki/File:JapaneseAmericansChildrenPledgingAllegiance1942-2.jpg.)

Eleanor Roosevelt holds a newsprint copy of the Universal Declaration in Spanish. Photograph, November 1949. Courtesy of the Franklin D. Roosevelt Library website and WikiMedia Commons. (Retrieve from: https://secure.wikimedia.org/wikipedia/en/wiki/File:EleanorRooseveltHumanRights.png.)

Index

Page numbers in **Bold** represent figures.